My Egypt Archive

My Egypt Archive

A L A N   M I K H A I L

Yale UNIVERSITY PRESS

New Haven and London

Published with assistance from the foundation established in
memory of Calvin Chapin of the Class of 1788, Yale College; from
the Charles S. Brooks Publication Fund; and from the Kingsley
Trust Association Publication Fund established by the Scroll and
Key Society of Yale College.

Yale University Press books may be purchased in quantity for
educational, business, or promotional use. For information, please
e-mail sales.press@yale.edu (U.S. office) or sales@yaleup.co.uk
(U.K. office).

Set in Minion type by Integrated Publishing Solutions.
Printed in the United States of America.

ISBN 978-0-300-26099-1 (hardcover : alk. paper)
Library of Congress Control Number: 2022934785
A catalogue record for this book is available from the British
Library.

This paper meets the requirements of ANSI/NISO Z39.48-1992
(Permanence of Paper).

10 9 8 7 6 5 4 3 2 1

My Egypt Archive

1

Note on Sources

Historians go to archives. Day after day, hour upon hour, year following year, we, the scavenging historians, venture into thickets of paper seeking words generally not produced for us, words hidden, forgotten, discarded. "'Going to the archives,'" Michel de Certeau correctly observes, "is the statement of a tacit law of history."

Between 2001 and 2010, I worked in the enormous state bureaucracy of the Egyptian National Archives (Dār al-Wathā'iq al-Qawmiyya). The threshold for entry into the guild of professional historians was years of archival research, and I went to Cairo to do the research that would make me a historian. Working to become a historian meant inhabiting a government institution, some might say *the* government institution of Egypt. Within the gray walls of the archive's three behemoth Cold War–era buildings lived Egypt—its past in the millions of records it held and its present in the churn of the thousands of people who worked there. In the 2000s, I breathed in the archive's rhythms, comporting myself to its functions, under-standing it, witnessing people's interactions with one another and with the lurching Egyptian state. Like everyone who worked in the archive, every day I lumbered through Cairo traffic to arrive at around 10:30 a.m. I would sit at my desk for as long as I could, usually until sometime between 3 and 5 p.m. My clos-est community in those years was the administrative staff of the archive and my fellow researchers.

The ten years I worked in the archive not only made me a historian of Egypt; they also made a revolution that toppled the Egyptian government. Through thousands of quotidian acts of power and oppression, the state's economic failings and lack of political and social accountability bore down on indi-viduals and families, communities and relationships. Living and working inside a state institution before the revolution, I ex-perienced how the state cultivated its own demise. *My Egypt Archive* chronicles the decade before 2011, offering a singular perspective on one of the century's major political upheavals. It tells two inextricably bound stories: a historian learns the craft of history, as the society around him swells toward its own remaking.

This book thus embodies the dual meaning of the Greek root of archive, *arche:* both a beginning and a domain for the exercise of power. I understand the archive as a place of be-coming—the creation of historical narratives, the development of my personal identity as a historian, and the emergence of a rebellious politics—and as an arena of interpersonal, govern-mental, and intellectual power maneuvering. The reading room of the archive was not a neutral space of objective knowledge production, a romanticized sanctuary of quiet reflection and thought. It was a place where reputation, status, nationality, power, and experience were the coin of the realm. In this way it was very much an Egyptian space. As throughout Egyptian society, in the archive one had to learn how to navigate particular cultural, gendered, religious, and social mores. The story of the archive is therefore not only an account of a repository of paper, of the historian's law. In miniature, it encompasses the whole of Egyptian society.

As an Egyptian American, I possessed both an insider's knowledge and an outsider's status. I was born to Egyptian parents in Texas, fantastically enough about fifteen miles south of the town of Egypt, Texas. They had immigrated to the United States in the mid-1970s, thanks in large part to the Immigration and Nationality Act of 1965. Most of my extended family remained in Egypt. We visited nearly every summer, spoke constantly with our relatives and friends in Egypt, and received an Egyptian newspaper once a week. My father passed on to me his love of the culture and secular nationalist politics of Egypt in the 1950s and 1960s. I thus grew up American but with one foot in Egypt, and Egyptian with both feet in the United States. I was in some ways orthogonal to these two cultures that made me, comfortable in but not fully belonging to either and an observer, imbiber, and critic of both.

Events in the Middle East marked the timeline of my life in America. I was born just after the oil crisis of the 1970s and the Camp David Accords and in the midst of the Iranian hostage crisis. Watching the Palestinian Intifada on American television as an eight-year-old in the late 1980s is one of my earliest memories of political consciousness. Then came the Gulf War in the early 1990s, the sanctions the United States imposed on Iraq, and soon the Oslo Accords in the mid-1990s. I started college in 1997, taking as many Middle Eastern history courses as I could, trying to put some meat on the skeleton of my understanding of the region.

I entered graduate school in 2001. Just a few weeks into my first semester, I received a phone call early on the morning of September 11, well before I would need to head to my Arabic class, telling me to turn on the television. The 2000s—the decade in which the United States invaded Afghanistan and Iraq, the decade in which Islam became America's foremost enemy—was the decade in which I became a professional historian of the Middle East, spending most of those years living in and traveling around the region for study and research.

When I went to the Egyptian National Archives for the first time in 2001, I was determined to assert my independence from my family and the Egypt I had come to know as a child. I was in Cairo for professional reasons, I had my own apartment, and I forged my own social network. I made Egypt my own in the 2000s. Although I can almost "pass" as an Egyptian, and often do—I speak Arabic fluently, know the country, understand its jokes and habits, possess Egyptian citizenship, can dress suitably, and so on—in many ways I am not and can never be Egyptian. The fact that my family was Christian imposed another impediment to a sense of fully belonging to Egypt's dominant Muslim culture.

In the archive, my Egyptianness provided benefits denied to other foreigners: not only giving me access to documents but also social acceptance, entrée into conversations, and invitations to events and other gatherings. At the same time, the distance imposed by my Americanness always remained. In Egypt, uncertainties about my loyalties regularly surfaced. I constantly fielded questions about which country I liked more, which was "better." Did I feel more Egyptian or more American? Even if America was richer and more comfortable, didn't I prefer the culture of family and togetherness in Egypt? The United States suffered from swine flu in 2009; Egypt, people in the archive claimed with pride, did not. Most crucially, would I marry an Egyptian or an American? Some in

the archive found the Americanness of my Egyptianness suspect. Most simply saw it as a curiosity.

For me, Egypt was always familiar and yet still distant. I
had the access that comes with intimacy, knowledge, experience, and feeling but also the space to approach the country as
an outside observer would. My dual insider-outsider position-
ality is, I believe, both a reason why I became a historian of
Egypt and, I would offer, an advantageous relationship for a
historian to have to his materials—deeply ensconced and pos-
sessing a tactile, almost instinctual sensibility, yet also removed,
skeptical, questioning. I was not so naïve, or solipsistic, as to
think that I would somehow find clues to my own identity in
eighteenth-century court records. Yet something drew me to
the Egyptian archive. Its infinitude of possibilities offered endless opportunities to find what I was searching for—acceptance,
community, love—to impose order on the unordered. This act
was for me both personal and an embodiment of the historian's craft—ascribing logic and structure to the inchoate and
messy. As we all strive to understand our complex personal
identities in the rush and roar of life, so too the historian attempts to identify cause and effect, create chronologies, and
sequence events from the deluge of what happened.

The national archive is one of the most privileged perches
from which to view Egypt's political history. As a repository of
the paper record bureaucracies make, it is the nerve center of
any government. As complicated and policed as the Egyptian
archive is, it remains the central storehouse of the history of
the Egyptian state. Here more than anywhere else is where the
story of Egypt resides. Custodian of memory, the archive is at
the same time an organic part of Egypt's contemporary state
bureaucracy. People come to work here every day; this buzzing
bureaucratic beehive constantly moves and categorizes paper;

it lists and lurches even as it supports an entire community
of researchers, administrators, and functionaries. In the three
hundred years between the eighteenth-century Egypt I was
studying on the page and the living, breathing Egypt in the
room, I was observing different castings of the same state. I was
at once historian, observer, participant, and ethnographer. I
wrote several histories from the sources that were laid out on
the desk in front of me. Unlike those books, this one looks up
from the documents, focusing not on the Egypt on my desk
but the one around it.

My Egypt Archive is based on a journal I kept during those
years. In it, I worked out ideas that came to me while reading
archival documents and reflecting on experiences I had in the
archive and in Cairo more generally. This writing was sometimes part of the intellectual work of fleshing out and testing
historical ideas, but it quickly became a space of feeling, reflection, and aspiration. Alongside ideas for articles and future
research projects—and, of course, the normal stuff of personal
writing: family and relationships, longings and emotions—I
sometimes described what had happened in the archive that
day: peculiar events, conversations, or notable experiences. In
holding back any outward expression of those thoughts and
feelings, I had acclimated to the Egyptian politics of self-cen-
sorship. As in the rest of Egypt, in the soft dictatorship of the
archive no one reveals one's genuine reactions for fear of re-
prisal. Only in the intensely private and personal inside of my
journal would I try to make sense of the outside world of Egypt
and its archive. I did not think much of those pages when I
wrote them—they were not written for an archive—and after-
ward mostly forgot about them.

They came back to me in that stupendously hopeful
month of January 2011, when, at great personal risk, hundreds
of thousands of Egyptians endeavored to wrest control of their

country from the hands of the oligarchy that had ruled them since Hosni Mubarak came to power in 1981 (or, some might say, since Gamal Abdel Nasser's revolution in 1952). In Egypt, and elsewhere in the region, the so-called Arab Spring took aim at the repression, stagnation, and depression that had been building for decades. The economies of most Middle Eastern countries suffered under the obligations of corrosive deals with the International Monetary Fund and the World Bank, the global economic recessions of the early and late 2000s, and the corruption and nepotism of their leaders. In Egypt by 2011 the result was a cavernous wealth gap between the rich and the majority of the population, already poor, who found them- selves growing ever poorer and more underserved, even as they saw a small over-class living like kings and queens. More people grew discontented and angry, spurring more critique, which the regime met with more repression—including tor- ture and summary executions—all relentlessly intensifying so- cial tensions across Egypt.

When the protests broke out in Cairo, I was in New Haven, very far away, feeling alone and disconnected from Egypt after nearly a decade of living and working there. Having only just arrived in southern Connecticut, in the first real winter of my life, I consumed all I could about what was happening in Egypt, a place I cared deeply about personally and professionally. I streamed television online, followed Twitter and Facebook, called as many people as I could, and contemplated flying back to Egypt to be a part of what was clearly a ground shift.

Desperate for connection, the kind I had sought before in the archive, I thought to search for the journal that was now at the back of a closet where I had thrown things I didn't know where to put after moving from California, where I had writ- ten my dissertation. I found and read it for the first time that January, devouring it with a completely different set of eyes

from the pair that had produced it. With the dissociating distance of time, I read it as a record not just of personal experiences and a workbook of historical reflection but as a documentary record of Egypt in the years leading up to January
2011. In this archive of my life, I had chronicled the life of the
archive. I had compiled a catalog of the political, social, and
economic forces behind the revolt as they had played out
through my local world of the archive's bureaucratic hierarchy:
conversations with fellow researchers about their lives and families, tensions between bureaucrats, the untenability of living
in Egypt on a government salary, understandable anger at a
state that did not support its citizens, the criminal corruption
of Egypt's leaders, the political uses of state violence, failing
social services, a lack of education and employment opportunities, gaping wealth disparities. I read my journal, in other
words, as we always do historical materials—through the lens
of the present. Having studied and contemplated the craft of
history for many years by this point, I understood that history
is always as much—perhaps even more—about the present as
it is about the past. In 2011, I read my journal of the 2000s not
through the eyes of an aspiring historian drudging in the archive every day but through those of the Egyptians I was now
following from afar, the protesters in Tahrir Square hoping to
remake their society.

This book, then, is at once both a portrait of the historian
as a young man and a chronicle of Egypt before the revolution,
one written from inside the state. I am a character in this drama,
and I strive throughout to make myself—historian, researcher,
author, person—an object of inquiry. In stepping outside myself, I do not shy away from exposing my vulnerabilities, foibles,
insecurities, and failings, or describing my work, choices, prog-
ress, and desires. My method is one of critical self-abnegation
in the service of cultural analysis. The same politics of modern

capitalism, discipline, bureaucracy, and empire that produced the revolutionary conditions of 2011 produced me as a proper striving historical subject. I therefore analyze myself not for my own sake but to grasp the nature of a particular alloy: one composed of Egyptian culture and politics, the making of the historian, and the act of archival research. To become a historian, I first had to pass through the archive's security protocol. Once inside, I navigated a politics of photocopying and reputation, pen usage and deference. I adapted to the shift schedule of the administrative workday, construction work in the archive's reading room, and the endless snafus of government inefficiencies. I witnessed the treatment of bureaucrats and researchers of different social stations, several dramatic archival thefts, administrative turnover, the upheavals sparked by the impending visit of Egypt's first lady, and the transformations wrought by the arrival of computers. All these events shaped me as a person and a historian. All reveal something of how the function of Egypt's state bureaucracy and of Egyptian society led to the social and political ruptures of 2011. Against the vagaries, injustices, low-frequency frustrations, aspirations, and rhythms of life in Egypt in the 2000s, all evince the fused politics and practices of the double meaning of the phrase "making history."

None, though, appear anywhere else on paper, in any of the historical works I or others have written. Behind the thousands of words historians write lie years of archival research, personal relationships with archivists and other historians, lost pages, research leads that fizzle out, and all the messy experiences of daily life. The near complete invisibility of these visceral experiences of archival research seems to me a misreflection of the historian's craft and a missed opportunity to understand how research is done and the political and personal contexts in which it is done. My experiences of archival research shaped me—bodily, intellectually, culturally, politically—and, therefore, shaped the histories I wrote. Yet they are nowhere to be found in the final product of my books and articles. They are the unseen sequence of events that occurred parallel to, and directly because of, the histories I published. As a kind of autononfiction, *My Egypt Archive* dwells in this antimatter, which lies behind everything historians do, bringing into focus the shadow stories of how history is really made.

In doing so, it offers a novel historical methodology through the many questions it asks. What are the historical and personal circumstances in which history is produced? How and why do they matter? What is the relationship between the immediate fleeting moment of intellectual production and its final form on a page? How can we recover that initial experience of insight, and how does understanding it shape our sense of the historical craft and historical consciousness? Where do archival experiences go? What might they mean? Was there a relationship between my stiff back and the imperial firmans I was transcribing when I ached? The past is not only what we read in the archive but also what we felt, heard, smelled, thought, and did in the archive. What is the utility of writing a history of the experience of doing history? Indeed, where does the experience of *doing* history go when *writing* history? How, more abstractly, do the conditions of the production of history affect the history that is produced? For me, answering these questions lays bare not only how historians work and how supposedly objective history is made but also how the place of that production—in this case, Egypt—functions.

Yet, even as an institutional history of and in one site in an authoritarian regime in the Global South, this book's arguments extend to processes of archival research broadly. As noted in the final chapter, a robust scholarly literature interrogates the multiple complex relationships among archives, the writing of history, state development, subjectivity, national histories, class politics, access, and suppression. Much of this concerns Europe and little of it addresses these questions in the context of an authoritarian state that maintains a theoretically public archive that aims nevertheless to limit the kinds of questions researchers might ask and their access. Another body of scholarship cited in the final chapter informs this work: the critical anthropology of ethnography and ethics. In the ways that anthropologists have usefully questioned their field's theories and practices, I reflexively probe how the processes, circumstances, methods, and theoretical underpinnings of historians' research should and can be critically considered, unsettled, and, ultimately, productively incorporated in their scholarship.

That quintessential product of archival research, the endnote—lying cold in the recesses of a book's back pages, with its category headings and page numbers—can never fully capture or express the blood-pumping emotional and intellectual experiences that produced it, arguably as historically consequential as the estate inventory or letter it cites. The note manifests the multiple meanings of the Greek *arche*. It references the original sources on which understanding is based and, defending its territory on the page, demarcates a space to order and present information. *My Egypt Archive* strikes at the authority of the note. It argues that the note, that archival ambassador, conceals multiple histories of the actual creation of historical scholarship.

Because of state censorship, the Egyptian National Archives holds no materials for the period after the 1940s. The official repository of Egyptian state documents has nothing to say about Egyptian history since 1952, or, perhaps more accurately, chooses not to release any documents about that period. Instead, the state manipulates histories of itself, creating certain triumphalist narratives and suppressing others. The politics of the archive are a crucial weapon for any state. Therefore, to write the history of modern Egypt—one not produced as official propaganda—one must turn to sources other than those generated by the state. This does not make history impossible, of course, but it makes it limited, challenging, and of a particular tenor. Gaining entry to the Egyptian National Archives has always been difficult, but the years since 2011 have seen a drastic curtailment of access. Working outside the organs of the state, several heroic efforts—those of the Mosireen Collective, for example—have endeavored to collect and archive materials from the 2011 uprising and after so that future historians will be able to narrate those momentous events based on contemporary materials. While today's historians lament the absence of sources from the period since the 1940s, the unofficial archivists of the present strive to overcome future lacunae by collecting now.

In the face of these multiple challenges for the telling of modern Egyptian history, one of my aspirations for *My Egypt Archive* is that it may serve as a necessary record of its time, a sliver of a replacement archive of Egypt in the 2000s, a stay against the official version of that decade. Without a radical change in Egyptian politics, no official archives of the 2000s will ever be made accessible to researchers. If anything, the longer censorship continues, the more difficult access will become. In the absence of the normal stuff of historical inquiry— minutes of meetings, governmental budgets, official correspondence, and the like—we are left to seek out other sources to tell the history of Egypt. This book is one such documentary source, idiosyncratic and personal no doubt, individual and eccentric, but a historical source nonetheless. *My Egypt Archive* is an archive of Egypt in the 2000s, an archive of the archive, an archive of histories usually kept hidden.

2

Contents

In Egypt in the 2000s, fences, guardrails, barricades, and walls subjugated the landscape. The denser Cairo and other major cities became, the more highly demarcated and then guarded their spaces proved. The logic of security dominated. Against a perceived unruliness of possibility, the government monitored, surveilled, and brandished military-grade weapons in public spaces. The only thing more protected than space in Egypt was information. As an official government institution dedicated to information about the state, the Egyptian National Archives was thus a highly securitized space.

The archive lies in a district of Cairo known as Bulaq, a stretch of coastline along the eastern bank of the Nile that urban engineers reclaimed from the river in the early nineteenth century to allow merchant ships to dock and unload their goods. In a place as old as Cairo, Bulaq represents quite a young part of the city. In the 1980s and 1990s, as Egypt liberalized its economy and more and more money poured in from

the Gulf, Bulaq grew in popularity as a neighborhood for up-
market retail stores, soaring apartment towers, glitzy office
buildings, and American-style malls. It offered views of the
river and the city to the south and proximity to downtown.
Driving north from central Cairo up the corniche past the offices of Egyptian National Television, the foreign ministry, and
the Conrad Hotel—a luxury member of the Hilton group—
one arrives at the archive. Beyond, within walking distance, sit
the Sawiris Towers, a complex that houses an upscale mall,
swanky residences, and the offices of the Sawiris family of companies, one of Egypt's richest conglomerates.

Against these capitalist turrets of glass and steel, the archive cuts quite a contrast. It is a rectangular block, short and
wide. The soot and grime of Cairo's pollution—car traffic never
stops on the corniche—long ago painted over the four stories
of its once off-white façade. The archive itself fills only the
southern part of this elongated structure. More than half of the
building houses the Egyptian National Library (Dār al-Kutub
al-Qawmiyya) with its large collection of books, periodicals,
and manuscripts. Library and archive each have their own
entrance.

Behind the archive building and the row of massive structures that line the corniche, Bulaq sprawls away from the river
to the east. A poor area of Cairo, like countless others of its
neighborhoods, Bulaq's renown comes from its textile and
clothing stores and its metal and wood workshops. As in many
parts of the developing world, the rich in Cairo live on top of
the poor, the glitter of their wealth blinding them to what lies
outside their windows.

As soon as the area of Bulaq was reclaimed from the
river, early nineteenth-century Cairenes rushed to build on
this fresh land. But because the ground had not yet dried and

hardened enough to provide a proper foundation for building, many of the first structures toppled. Today, the fact that this land recently sat under water plays a crucial role in the life of the archive. Because the water table remains high, the soil underneath the archive is sodden. In Cairo's heat, this creates an emanating mugginess at the bottom of the building. Moisture, obviously, is one of paper's primary enemies, and, indeed, Bulaq's humidity has ruined volumes of archival material over the years, since the storage areas lack environmental controls. Furthermore, large tracts of the basement have never been finished and remain to this day damp exposed earth. I asked about these areas once and was told that one day they would be paved over to enlarge the basement's storage capacity. Thus, within steps of Egypt's paper heritage—documents that exist nowhere else in the world—dank earth steams.

Between the street and the building was a large black wrought-iron fence. On the inside of this one of Egypt's millions of border markers, two paths led into the archive. To the left, three steps led down to a small door. This rather nondescript opening served as the entrance for the archive's bureaucrats. To the right, up a large flight of black stone steps, researchers, visitors, and higher-ups in the archive's administration entered the building. Above the doors hung a large metal sign with the name of the archive in Arabic calligraphy. Before entering, one enjoyed a view of the Nile and the island of Zamalek. Looking down over the low walls of this elevated platform, one saw a small green space where lemon trees, tulips, and gardenia bushes rose up between empty chip bags, bits of newspaper, and a regular group of street cats fighting and playing. Between the two entrances was a driveway reserved for high administrators to park their cars. A group of government workers patrolled this courtyard, almost as police, waiting to open the black iron fence's large gate upon the arrival of an important person, so that he—or rather, his chauffeur— might drive in and park.

The spatial casting of these separate entrances reinforced Egypt's social and economic hierarchy, concretizing the segregation of classes in the archive, as in all government institutions. Everyone knew his or her place in the system. If the impossible occurred and somehow one forgot one's station, or, even more shockingly, if someone resisted, the world around wrenched the proper order back into place. Government bureaucrats, who earned a measly two to four hundred pounds a month, found themselves literally looking up at those using the main entrance, a threshold they could never cross. Upward mobility proved impossible.

The double doors of the archive's main entrance usually stayed open to the street. Although it made the building noisy, this routine allowed Cairo's generally comfortable temperatures to pass inside and facilitated a free flow of arrivals and exits. As a researcher, I almost always entered through these doors. One time, though, I used the workers' doorway on purpose, just to see what it was all about. Bucking standard procedure—by definition a problem, but especially so in Egypt—I was met at the door and asked what I was doing there. Given the camaraderie I had built up with many of the workers over my years in the archive, I felt comfortable enough to joke around. I told them I was tired of being a historian and wanted to be a bureaucrat instead. They laughed and, to their credit, played along, showing me where to sign and clock in for the day. Government workers, who represented the majority of the people entering and working in the building each day, were the most surveilled group in the archive, as they are across Egypt's countless bureaucratic structures. Nasser had guaranteed every Egyptian a government job, but it came with no guarantee of respect.

In the age of Mubarak, these assurances of employment had eroded. Now one generally needed connections to secure government employment, and contracts were often temporary and easily terminated. Higher-ups closely monitored the lower ranks, in part because they received wages from the state but mostly because Egypt's stratified class system had etched in stone a reputation for this still-majority of Egypt's workforce: they were seen as lazy, inefficient, dishonest, or even possibly thieving, if the opportunity presented itself. As a researcher, I could pretend to use their entrance; they could never pretend to use mine.

When workers entered the building's lowest level, they were required to check their personal items. A bureaucrat who monitored a wall of open storage shelves gave each worker a numbered card matching the number of the cubby shelf where his or her personal effects would sit for the day. After clocking in with a traditional punch clock, workers slotted their time cards into a large, gray iron shelving unit. Like the cubby section, the clocking-in area was the domain of the bureaucrat in charge of that procedure. In the vast, intricate machinery of the Egyptian state, everyone specialized in a single task.

Upon stepping through the doors at the top of the black stone steps, you entered a large lobby area. The bureaucrat sitting behind the security desk—nearly always Ahmed, a burly, jovial man whose appearance matched his work—asked who you were and where you were going and then entered your personal information in one of his many large leatherbound registers. Compiling his own daily archive of sorts, he first recorded the researcher's permit number. After even just a few weeks of trust-building, however, Ahmed, instead of going through the trouble of actually looking at the permit card himself, simply asked you to tell him the number. Many researchers had long since lost or misplaced their cards and had been entering for years in this fashion. Ahmed also asked for a form of official personal identification. Egyptian citizens normally presented their national identification card or driver's license and foreigners their passport. From these documents, Ahmed completed the rest of his entry in the register: the researcher's address, identification document number, and the time of arrival. While you worked in the archive, Ahmed kept possession of your government-issued ID—of much more importance than an archival permit, since one needed such official identification to do much of anything in Egypt.

I am an Egyptian citizen and possess the standard identification card. This fact produced much confusion and consternation for Ahmed. He knew I was American, lived in the United States, and had come from abroad to do research. I had an accent in Arabic and acted very obviously American to him—a source of much amusement. Being considered charming or funny of course helped in many social situations. I was always wary of this professionally, though, and no doubt overcompensated in my attempts to be the dour, serious historian. I told Ahmed of my Egyptian parents and family in Egypt, and my identification card clearly showed that I was a citizen, yet he insisted that I should use my American passport to register at the archive. He would always enter my address not as the one listed on my card but as a "hotel in Zamalek," the tony district on the island across from the archive popular with tourists. Ahmed and I liked each other, but he could not accept that I was an Egyptian citizen. My culture, it seemed, made my citizenship an impossibility.

In return for your government-issued ID, Ahmed gave you a numbered plastic card. In theory, your card reflected the order in which you entered the archive that day: the first researcher was supposed to receive card one, the twelfth number twelve, and so on. Rarely did this happen in practice. The plastic cards lived strewn in a drawer of Ahmed's desk that hung permanently open. Every morning Ahmed tried to put them in order, after the jumble in which they were returned the previous day, but inevitably he became too distracted or bored to carry this through. Who, honestly, would care? Usually he got close enough that the first five researchers received a card numbered between one and five. Ahmed threw all the passports and identification cards he collected into the same broken drawer.

Opposite Ahmed's security desk was one of the few real public spaces in the archive: a lobby with two sitting areas. The one closest to the desk consisted of a glass coffee table and three chairs upholstered in red with large holes in their seats exposing the foam interior, one of them missing an armrest. On the other side of a few columns, the second sitting area had a long black plastic couch, two more red chairs, and another glass coffee table. A pay phone on the wall demarcated the sitting areas, and a large framed reproduction of a fifteenth-century world map hung above the first. The marble surface of the first floor featured the same black and white geometric design as every other floor of the archive.

With numbered plastic card in hand, you made your way into the building via a long entranceway between the public areas and the security desk. (On special occasions, such as the visit of an important government official, a red carpet was unfurled along its length.) To the left was a flight of stairs leading up to the reading room and administrative offices on the second floor or down to the lowest level of the building, the level where the employees entered, clocked in, and stored their personal items, and where most archival materials were housed. Researchers descended to this level only to pay the central cashier for photocopies and other services. If you bypassed the stairs and continued straight back on the entrance level, you reached an area devoted partly to the repair of registers and documents and partly to storage. To the right, opposite the stairs, a conference room offered space for meetings and exhibitions. Near the stairs were the archive's two elevators. Bureaucrats whose job required them to go up and down the floors of the archive did their best to ensure that at least one elevator always functioned.

At the top of the stairs, on the second floor, to the left, sat a man. I never knew his name or understood his job. He sat there every day, sometimes eating or talking with someone, always watching who came up and down the stairs and in and out of the elevator, his chair perfectly positioned to see both points of access to the second floor. I eventually came to assume that this *was* his job: surveyor of second-floor arrivals.

Immediately opposite this man, to the right of the stairs, were the always closed doors of two nearly sacred offices. Together, these doors exercised a politics of unattainability regularly practiced in Egypt—dangling in front of one's face what one could never acquire. The Sawiris Towers did it in Bulaq; Mercedes-Benzes did it driving through Cairo's streets; these doors did it on the second floor of the archive. Behind one door was the photocopy department, a space only the most favored of researchers could hope to enter. Its plaque taunted me every day I passed it, as I coveted what it hid inside. Across from this door, a suite of offices belonged to the director of the archive. Large windows on either side of the closed door allowed one to see inside this almost otherworldly space: carpeted, air conditioned, with many windows overlooking the Nile. A receptionist sat in a pleasant waiting area with plants and magazines, and the suite included a small kitchen for making tea and coffee. The people who used that door seemed almost of a different species than the rest of us. The men wore suits and the women designer clothing. Clean shoes evidenced class and probably a driver. Most researchers and government employees never had reason to enter that area, but, through those windows, we saw it every day. Needless to say, this was by design: an ostentatious display of what belonged to the few and was denied to the many.

If you continued to the left of the stairs, away from the closed doors, you entered the main area of the second floor, which was dominated by a little café. Here researchers and others took breaks, drank tea and coffee, smoked, ate lunch, and generally relaxed, chatting and joking with friends and colleagues. Employees would often take advantage of the café's chairs to sit for breaks throughout the day. Up to forty people could be gathered here at any given time, and loud talking, laughter, and smoke wafted out from this central space to the various offices and departments surrounding it. These included the archive's small library, which housed dictionaries, encyclopedias, and other reference works, as well as theses and dissertations written from research in the archive's collection. These latter materials were especially valuable, as they had been produced in universities all over Egypt. You could read dissertations from small universities very far away—say, from towns like Qina or Ismailiyya—that were difficult to find since they existed only in those universities' libraries and in these copies that the authors usually gave to the national archives. Government employees considered working in this room a luxury, as it was generally quieter and less trafficked than most other sections of the archive—hence, there was less work to do. Its lights stayed dimmed, adding to its calm and soothing feel. A nearby room housed periodicals and other printed materials, mostly late nineteenth- and early twentieth-century newspapers.

Opposite the library, a narrow hallway led to the second floor's bathrooms. They always seemed to be under repair, often closed, with large sacks of sand stacked between the doors of the men's and women's rooms. The banging and hammering of repairmen regularly reverberated from inside. When available, the men's room was almost always wet underfoot from men splashing water onto their arms and legs to wash before prayer. Over the course of the day, the floor grew puddled and muddy. Bathroom stalls offered a unique space in the archive, the only place in the entire building where one could be completely alone—a fact that goes a long way in explaining why the bathroom became a preferred site for attempting the theft of archival materials.

On the edge of the second floor's common area, across from the café, was the secured storage room known as *al-amanat,* where researchers were required to leave their bags, books, and other personal effects while using archival materials. Similar in concept and form to the area where the workers stored their things when entering the archive, but serving only tens of researchers rather than hundreds of workers, the room seemed to be a converted closet, with a tiny desk, a wall of small shelves, and one easily locked door. This storage room maintained its own independent registering process. You first placed your personal effects in an empty cubbyhole, leaving with them the plastic card given to you by Ahmed. The card number was then recorded in a register—the same sort Ahmed used—by the person working in the storage area that day, usually a woman named Jehan. Jehan then wrote your name and time of entry in her register and handed you another plastic card with another number on it. She recorded this number too.

Once your belongings were secured, you could pass through the last door off the second floor's lobby area—the reading room, the researcher's inner sanctum, the archival temple's holy of holies. This ultimate destination of the historian represents the space in which humans become historians. Transformations happen here, changes I had only heard about before. Without the reading room, no archives. Without archives, no historians. Without historians, no history. The space possesses the mystery of the sacred, much discussed and contemplated, conceptualized and constructed, rumored and feared, only glimpsed and experienced after one has proved oneself worthy and ready. Researchers like me traveled from other continents for this place, spending thousands of dollars to be here, forming lives around our physical presence in the reading room. Crossing its threshold for the first time felt like a larval transmogrification. With fitting trepidation, I knew—*knew*—I was about to become a new person, to molt from student to historian, shedding the skin of youth to wrap myself in brittle archival pages. Like so many, I would spend the greater part of my time in the archive in the reading room, hour after hour, day after day, month after month.

Its doors opened directly onto the café, ensuring that much of the noise and cigarette smoke seeped inside. The hallowed space of the reading room proved surprisingly unadorned and simple. Dull walls and a greenish-gray carpet with many stains and rips greeted you in the small lobby beyond the room's wooden double doors. Directly across from the doors, three long tables arranged in an L sagged under the weight of four computers, the only ones in the reading room. Three seemed permanently idle; the other was often turned on in the afternoon, for what purpose I did not know. A group of government employees would sometimes play solitaire—together—on this computer. There did not seem to be any regulations about the use of the computers. People mostly avoided them.

Continuing past them into the main area of the reading room, your field of vision was dominated by a long table to the left, where the high priestess of the reading room sat with her staff. Researchers, whose destiny lay in the decisions made at this desk, stopped here first, generally bowing their heads in deference as they placed the plastic card Jehan had given them in a small box on this desk. All research materials currently in the reading room rested on the three long brown shelves behind the desk. It was up to you, not a member of the reading room staff, to retrieve your daily research materials from those shelves. You walked sheepishly around the desk, behind the watchful female guardians who protected them, careful not to disturb anyone or anything or create suspicion. They always knew who possessed what. On this desk, too, you wrote requests for materials and conducted any other business related to research in the reading room. It represented the room's central nervous system.

Opposite the watchful eyes at the front of the room were twenty-four wooden desks arrayed in four rows of six. The arrangement mirrored that of a school classroom. Each desk was large enough to accommodate two chairs, though more than one person at a desk was prohibited except on those rare days when the number of researchers created a shortage of space or when two people were working together on an authorized project. On most days, anywhere from ten to twenty researchers visited the reading room.

Where you sat conveyed important information about your place in the reading room's order. Each desk in the four-by-six grid held advantages and disadvantages, and the choice of where to place yourself was a complicated algorithm of balancing lighting against temperature, respect against trust, routine against noise. Some researchers preferred to be close to their friends. Others, creatures of habit, having found a desk they liked—or, superstitiously, one that had produced a wonderful find—chose to stick to it as best they could (seating was first come, first served). For many, the choice was not so obvious. Sitting closer to the front of the room meant more direct exposure to the air conditioning units; in summer, competition for front-row desks was fierce. The lighting tended to be much better at the front of the room, which was desirable for some but not for all. The main disadvantage of being near the front was noise—the staff chatting and conducting the reading room's business and the bleed from the café just outside the door. But working in the back row, as far as possible from the gaze of the room's bureaucrats, raised suspicions. When you first began work in the archive, you were not allowed to sit in the back row. Only after a period of time and trust-building did this stricture loosen, and you could begin to move farther away from the main desk. Some of Egypt's most respected historians were denizens of the back row. On most days, I settled into the comfortable safety of the middle of the pack.

Behind the four rows of desks sat six microfilm readers. Unlike the desks, the readers faced the rear of the room. While at first glance this arrangement seemed to contradict the archive's logic of security, it in fact made sense, since you could not hide behind the tall back of the microfilm reader. All six of the readers usually worked. Every three weeks or so, a technician came to the reading room to clean and maintain them. With so much in the archive in need of attention—burned-out lights, broken windows, leaking ceilings—I never understood why the microfilm readers, of all things, received regular service.

To the left of the researchers' desks, a small nook housed an old beat-up metal desk and three bookcases with some of the reading room's few catalogs (the shelves at the front of the room held some, too). These bound registers, similar to those used to check people in to the archive and their belongings into storage areas, covered a minuscule speck of the archive's

holdings—a small sliver of nineteenth-century interdepart-
mental government correspondence—and employed a catalog
numbering system that had already changed three times. They
were rarely consulted; however, the staff reserved the metal
desk in this area precisely for the purpose of reading them.
Not a normal, wooden desk like the others, this one possessed
an aura of distinction. Part of its specialness derived from its
position directly across from one of the three air conditioning
units, which made it among the most chilled desks in the room.
Certain important people were often granted permission to sit
at this privileged, cooled, metallic desk for their regular work.
Rules, as they often did in Egypt, applied only to those who
could not bypass them.

To the right of the researchers stood a forest of card catalogs, twenty or so, taking up close to a fifth of the room. At
various points over the life of the archive, different directors
had attempted to organize parts of the collection, and these
card catalogs resulted from one such attempt. They mostly
contained small summaries in Arabic of nineteenth-century
Ottoman documents related to the reign of Muhammad 'Ali
and his family. Many working on the nineteenth century began
their research here; however, because of the multiple numbering systems used in the archive over the years, it often proved
difficult to correlate the information on a card to an actual
document. A system of conversion existed to get around this
problem, though it, too, was far from exact.

Wedged into the corner was a small desk where two lowly
governmental employees sat, waiting to be summoned by the
head of the reading room. Some used the space near this desk
to pray rather than going to the main prayer rooms—one for
men, one for women—on the top floor, directly above the reading room. To go upstairs, you took a small staircase located off
the short hallway leading to the bathroom. There was little be-

yond the prayer rooms on this floor, other than storage. In the ensconced securitized bureaucratic hierarchy that the physical structure of the archive so faithfully reproduced, governmental employees lay firmly at the bottom, administrators and researchers in the middle, and God above all.

3
Permissions

In the beginning was the permit, and the permit was not with me. Only with it in hand could one map and inhabit the space of the archive. The process of gaining permission to enter and use the archive immediately threw one into the teeth of Egyptian National Security (Amn al-Dawla or another of the security agencies, which one was never clear). After the staff of the archive vetted an application for research, it moved up to be assessed by an office of the national security apparatus. The same logic that erected barricades and put guns in the hands of police on Cairo's streets seeped into the construction of Egypt's history. For the historian, security, access, and permission stood as the requisite first steps into the craft. If one could not see documents, one could not write history. So much of the historical enterprise revolves around who can see what. The permit bluntly structured the potentials of the histories that could be written. Who had permission to narrate Egypt's past?

Nowhere was there a clear articulation of who would

gain access to the archive and who would not. Vagueness functioned as a deliberate and effective strategy across Egypt. The ambiguous notion of an Islamist terrorist threat or an imminent attack by Israel, for example, justified the maintenance of emergency rule for the whole of Hosni Mubarak's reign. A generalized sense of Egyptian amity meant that no one purchased car insurance because, in a nondescript way, Egyptians always did the right thing. In the archive, with no clear guidelines in place, the state could do what it liked, no questions asked, leaving one only to guess as to why a particular person received a permit and someone else not. Certain research areas were clearly off limits: topics related to foreign policy or Egypt's wars and most anything from the 1940s on—the period after the establishment of the state of Israel, the Egyptian Revolution of 1952, and the expansion of the state's machinery of security.

The best strategy for a researcher applying to work in the archive was to meet vagueness with vagueness. The more general a topic, the more innocuous it sounded. In this way, even from the moment of applying to access the archive, security concerns entered into the calculus of a historian's research. At the time I applied for my permit, I wanted to work on the history of medicine in eighteenth-century Egypt and so was instructed to write as my research topic "eighteenth- and nineteenth-century social history." Not only would this fuzziness seem ignorable but it would, in theory at least, not limit the kinds of sources I would be able to see in the archive, if I was allowed in at all. From California, I sent to a professor I knew in Cairo my application for a permit along with two passport-size photos, an official letter in Arabic and English from my thesis adviser (the more official-looking, the better) stating the purpose and title of my research project, and a copy of my Egyptian ID card. My professor friend wrote to tell me that all had been delivered and that we should inquire in six weeks or so.

When I arrived in Cairo six months later, my research permit was not yet ready. I landed in early summer, keen to begin my forays in the archive after years of preparation. I felt like a bucking bronco in the chute before the gate is flung open. I was ready to leap and smash my way through the archive. Beyond taking years of courses, reading everything I could about Egyptian history and the Egyptian National Archives, and preparing the documents I needed for my application, I had built my life around spending years in Cairo. I had left my university and department, moved out of my apartment, and said goodbye to my social network. My plan to be gone for at least two years precipitated a breakup with my girlfriend. I had come to graduate school to become a historian. Historians went to archives. However high the price of admission to the guild, I was, for better or worse, committed and ready to pay.

Having expected delay, bureaucracy's norm everywhere, I remained unperturbed that first summer. I concentrated on doing other things to prepare for my research. I reconnected with colleagues in Egypt, bought books, readjusted to life in the city, saw friends and family, and generally got my bearings. It was all thoroughly enjoyable. The archive loomed; I waited. In mid-July, nearly seven months after I had sent the application materials to my friend in Cairo, I learned my permit was ready. Elated by this news and relieved that the national security authorities found me unremarkable, I was facing a moment of truth. I found myself growing apprehensive. Retrieving the permit would mark the first time I entered the archive. I knew—well, at that point, hoped—I would be spending a lot of time in that building over the coming years. But what if I hated it? What if the people there hated me? Added to this general anxiety was the realization that I now had no excuse *not* to be in the archive. It was the reason I had come to Cairo, and it stood open. Being in Cairo for research but not being *in* the archive would eat at me.

Dutifully, I went to the archive to retrieve my permit without delay. I was scolded for entering the wrong way, through the workers' entrance—long before my bad joke—and then directed to the door at the top of the black stone steps. At the front desk, Ahmed (this was our first meeting) looked me up and down—though it was the peak of summer, I was wearing a sport coat and dress shoes to try to make a good first impression—and asked me what I wanted. With pride, I said I had a permit waiting for me. Ahmed made a phone call and then told me to go upstairs to the reading room. All extremely promising, I thought. I thanked him profusely and, pretending to know where to go, headed confidently for the stairs I saw beyond his desk. At the top, I scanned the scene in front of me, hoping for some direction. To my surprise, I saw a set of double doors on the far side of the café with a plaque next to them saying "reading room" (*qā'at al-baḥth*). There it was. Having crossed North America, the Atlantic, and the Mediterranean, I had arrived at this corner of Africa. After years of fetishization, preparation, mythology, anticipation, hope, and anxiety, I finally stood on the cusp of entering that place—*the archive.* I wanted to speed through this ominous portal to the other side as quickly as possible.

I pushed through the double doors for the first of what would become hundreds of times. I veered left, past the sagging computer tables, taking in the new terrain, and glimpsed the head bureaucrat sitting at her desk. Even at this first glance, it was obvious that she was the person who held my research permit, and hence my professional future, in her hands. I would come to know her very well over the years. I walked over, mulling the most appropriate way to greet her, asking myself how I could possibly not have thought about what I was going to say at this critical moment. Having reached her with no strategy, I smiled and greeted her very normally. I wanted nothing more than for her to like me. Intimidated, my pulse racing, I tried to engage her warmly, but she barely looked up, waving me to a broken metal chair with black upholstery. She shuffled through some papers underneath her desk, found my permit, and handed it to me, saying nothing. I am not sure what I imagined for this moment, but certainly something more than this. An anointing of historian's oil, perhaps? A ceremonial oath? A handshake? Finally being let in on the secrets all the other historians seemed to know? I looked at the permit for a few moments. Next to my picture, it listed my name, address, citizenship, and research topic. The topic read "the history of society in the eighteenth and nineteenth centuries." This pleased me with its broadness and encouraged my hope that I would be able to see the documents I wanted.

After a few moments perusing my new research permit, I looked up expectantly at my god incarnate. I smiled again nervously; she stared back at me blankly. As part of the ceremony, admittedly still unformed in my mind, of retrieving my permit and entering the archive for the first time, I imagined a welcome, a tour of the space, an explanation of research tools, or an official primer to the reading room. The eyes looking back at me seemed to say merely, "You are free to go." I gathered that if I wanted an introduction to the archive I would have to instigate it myself, and so, overly eager and against my better judgment, I asked her if there were catalogs I might consult or if she had any suggestions as to where I should begin. She looked at my permit again, to see what my topic was. She hesitated and then said that I probably would not find much in the archive. My heart sank. This remark did not bode well for my future in the reading room, as she alone determined what materials qualified as relevant to "my" topic. She suggested I go to the Egyptian National Library, which housed manuscripts and printed books. I would find much more there, she said. But in my still-forming historian's mind, archives—not manuscripts or books—represented the sine qua non of the stuff of history.

Although I did not know it at the time, my questions on that first day were sorely misplaced. The archive and, by extension, the government employees who worked there did not think in terms of research topics. The overriding logic of the archive was a bureaucratic and organizational one, laced through with security concerns. On that first day, I did not grasp how the institution of the archive worked and, more significantly, what this meant for the writing of history in Egypt. Instead of beginning with certain topics, problematics, people, or events, history in Egypt was most often written about archival units. The archive shaped history in direct ways. Historians wrote about the court records of a certain city or the administration of a government department. Theses and dissertations have titles like "The Court of Mansura" or "The Department of Housing." Given that the archive itself has no index to most of its collection, these works organizing and summarizing the records in an archival unit proved extremely useful as the sorts of research guides I had naïvely expected to exist. The question of where to look for sources on eighteenth-century medicine, or even eighteenth- and nineteenth-century social history, was therefore the wrong question to ask. As soon as I asked it, the head of the reading room likely began riffling through all of the archive's various collections and units in her head. Given that no archival heading was an obvious match for my stated interest, she told me I would find nothing on the topic. (Perhaps an additional factor was that fewer historians meant less work.) Most researchers in the Egyptian National Archives grabbed onto one archival unit like a vein of gold and mined it until it tapped out. To think in terms of topics rather than archival units ran counter to this logic, and I, therefore, had to learn how to translate my interests into an Egyptian archival language that would get me the documents I wanted. Only after working in the archive for a few months and after many conversations did I realize that I had to think in terms of local courts and governmental departments—to work with the bureaucratic designations of the archive itself.

What I did learn on my first day were some of the many rules. No pens, only pencils. No cell phone usage in the reading room. No notebooks, only loose sheets of paper. No food. No cameras. Research permits had to be renewed every year. I would also quickly grasp that the archive's rules about everything applied to nothing. Such exacting detail acted as a corollary to vagueness in Egypt. Both were mechanisms of state power. Rules existed for every detail of life (perhaps even put down in writing somewhere) and governed nearly every institution, business, restaurant, agency, household, and school. Egyptians like to joke that their bureaucracy is the world's oldest, at five thousand years. Yet ubiquitous as they were, most of Egypt's rules lay dormant, unknown, unenforced. The threat of enforcement, though, loomed at every moment. After years of smoking on the bus, one might suddenly be informed that smoking on the bus is illegal. But what about the previous five years when I smoked on the bus and no one seemed to care? Irrelevant. Many of the codified-though-never-enforced rules aimed at quite reasonable and important matters. One should indeed refrain from using a pen in an archive. Yet when you see most people using pens, you acclimate to the culture of pen usage (why them and not me?), only to be chastised later for using a pen in the archive. Egyptians overcame the crush-

ing avalanche of rules primarily by ignoring them. The rules
slowed society and one's life. Bypassing them was one of the
most efficient and productive means of greasing the wheels of
social and economic relationships.

 One day, a policeman stopped me for talking on my cell
phone while driving—technically a violation, though rarely enforced. Why uphold this rule on this day on this road? The
officer asked to see both of my licenses—my individual driver's license and the car's operating license (equivalent to its
registration). I handed them to him and he put them in his
pocket, informing me that I would have to go to a police station the following morning to pay a fine of one hundred pounds
before I could retrieve them. I grew agitated and annoyed and
told him that I was very busy the next day—I wasn't—and
would not be able to go to the station. Despite knowing the
futility of the question, I asked why he had stopped me out of
all the other millions of drivers talking on their phones. Why
selectively enforce the rules with me, I asked in my head. Pick
someone else! His blank stare clearly signaled what I already
knew I was to do in this situation. I gave him twenty pounds,
took back my licenses, and drove away.

 Egyptian law clearly states that talking on the phone while
driving is a violation, and, for the good of society, it should
be. The penalty for this infraction is one hundred pounds and
the seizure of one's licenses until the fine is paid. The officer
who took my licenses and I both knew why he had stopped
me. Such policemen made six hundred pounds a month, about
one hundred U.S. dollars—not enough to support a single person, let alone a family. Quite reasonably, they supplemented
their government income by collecting money from motorists
as they could. Some might call it a bribe, but it functioned more
as a means of economic redistribution in a corrupt system that
stole from the citizenry. From my perspective, the choice was

obvious. I was happy to give this poor man who stood in traffic all day twenty pounds rather than giving the Egyptian government one hundred pounds (and spending a few hours at a police station in the bargain). Bypassing the law benefited us both, though it did little to prevent people from using their phones while driving.

The same principle held in the archive. The nonenforcement of rules benefited both parties—worker and researcher. Renewing a permit every year proved a hassle for the researcher and a great deal of work for the archive's staff. What really was the big deal about using pens? Easier to let this go. Rules produced delay, hardship, and tedium. No one wants any of that. Moreover, the power to choose when rules apply, and to whom, represented a means of control for the authorities. Uncertainty about the timing and context of the application of existing laws kept everyone off balance, especially, of course, the weakest in society, who are always the most common targets of state power.

The ethos of Egyptian security embodied by endless selective rules, applications, permits, guards, locked doors, and security procedures manifested as well in the ways many Egyptians thought about history and its place in society. A conversation in the archive's small café years into my research made this very clear. A group of Egyptian researchers and another American graduate student and I were enjoying coffee around one of the glass-topped tables. At a certain point, one of the Egyptians turned to my American colleague and asked her why she worked on the history of Egypt. I could see that the question took her aback. Our Egyptian colleague meant nothing challenging or malicious by the question; she was genuinely curious: Why not study the history of America? After all, our Egyptian friend said, she was an American and America was her country. Was she not interested in writing the history of her own country? Why would she be drawn to a place so far away and different from America, a nation of which she was not even a part? Why care about the history of a country that was not your own?

The sentiments expressed in these questions reveal some of the ways Egyptians conceive of history and their responsibilities toward the past—*their* past. For most, Egypt had to be protected and cast in a positive light. The vagueness of the threats against Egypt demanded its defense. As in all national historiographies, some Egyptians wrote as crude nationalists; however, most did not. Nearly all, though, held on to some notion of Egyptian distinction, the idea that the specialness of Egypt required care and protection. With an air of suspicion, the Egyptian historian of Egypt wondered whether an American historian of Egypt could be trusted to understand and contribute to the project of the Egyptian nation. Did she subscribe to the same notion of history that most Egyptians did? Would she make Egypt look good or bad? At base, this was the question for most Egyptian historians. And until it was answered, the non-Egyptian historian had to be treated with caution. If she ultimately proved to be a friend of the nation, she would be lauded and admired, as Egyptian historians greatly prized those non-Egyptian historians who expressed intellectual sentiments supportive of a nationalist conception of Egypt's past. Non-Egyptians offering proof of Egypt's greatness strengthened the nation's case, allowing Egyptian historians to claim exoneration from the accusation of blind nationalism, which they understood some took as negative. The recognition of Egypt's glory by non-Egyptians, who had been born without any obligation toward Egypt, strengthened its standing as truth.

As an Egyptian American, I posed a challenge for the assessing of loyalties. In the archive, I was clearly a foreigner. I myself felt more American in Egypt than I ever did in the United

States. I had been born, educated, and inculcated in the United States, yet I felt culturally very Egyptian, was legally an Egyptian citizen, had family in Egypt, and knew the country well. Where did this place me in the eyes of my fellow researchers? Did my heritage mean I recognized the grandeur of Egypt more than other Americans did? Did I love Egypt? Was I writing Egyptian history as "my own" or not? Did the "Egyptian" blood coursing through my veins reveal to me things non-Egyptians could never understand? Or did the facts of my dual citizenship, American upbringing, and accent disqualify me from Egyptianness? What made one an Egyptian, anyway? To be accepted as a legitimate historian in Egypt, one had to prove one's allegiance. Being identifiably Egyptian, whatever that meant, helped. Evidencing fealty and love sealed it.

Partly in and partly out, I proved suspect. I viscerally reacted, and acted, against the game of nationalist history, no matter the nation. As best I could, I rejected the imposition on me of any unearned privileges that came from being whatever amount of Egyptian I was. I did not believe that one needed to be Egyptian—let alone an Egyptian nationalist—to be a historian of Egypt, any more than one needed to be American to be a historian of America or Thai to be a historian of Thailand. I fancied I could, in my naïve and small way, change how Egyptians, and others, viewed history. But who was I? Even as I felt myself the impostor Egyptian—never mind the impostor historian—oscillating between trying to be more Egyptian than American, more Egyptian than Egyptians, I strove to move beyond the frame of national history. This more than anything else made me a non-Egyptian historian in and of Egypt.

On my first day in the archive, I did not spend much time fretting about any of this. That would come later. For now, I had received my permit. I held it tight. I marked and celebrated this victory. As I left the archive for the first time, I profusely and deferentially thanked the reading room staff and all the bureaucrats I encountered as I collected my belongings and exited the building. On my way down the steps, I impatiently called my aunts to tell them I had secured my permit. I also called to thank the professor who had helped me get it. Excited and daunted, I began to think about how I would organize my research time. As archival researchers query themselves daily, I asked myself for the first time that day, "Will I go back tomorrow?"

4
Figures

The high priestess of the reading room had a name. This hierophant, who interpreted the workings of an invisible, inscrutable, capricious Egyptian god, alone descried the world for us researchers, shaping our futures and fates, giving and taking life as she was divinely tasked (or herself chose?). She, our conduit to the sacred, was Madam Amal.

Madam Amal had worked in the archive for years, having served as assistant to the former head of the reading room, a woman named Madam Sawsan, who had retired some eight or nine years previously. Like Hosni Mubarak, having put in her time as the number two, Madam Amal gladly took over the top position. Unlike Mubarak, however, she deserves our respect—an underprivileged, overworked woman in a sexist society, with little choice but to serve a system that repressed her, who earned a position of power through her skill and sheer force of will. The archive, like nearly every institution in Mubarak's Egypt, functioned as a dictatorship in miniature.

Such governance saturated all of Egyptian society, and thus in this fractal world of corrupt megalomaniacal power, where the tiniest scale replicated the overall structure, analyzing the smallest part illuminates the whole. Power was monopolized and centralized in a hierarchical system where one's station was fixed and mostly determinative of one's fate. The machine of social politics crushed any attempt to resist, change, or overcome it. Such an enormous, sprawling, seemingly infinite bureaucracy was embodied, perhaps paradoxically, in a single person. For the entirety of Egypt, this central pole was Hosni Mubarak. For researchers and workers in the reading room of the archive, it was Madam Amal—our Mubarak in miniature (though in contrast to Mubarak, she had a boss above her in the hierarchy, who exercised absolute power over her and everyone underneath her). Egypt's modern history has usually been organized around the persons of a few omnipotent men: Nasser, Sadat, Mubarak. In truth, one woman governed Egypt's history: Madam Amal.

Madam Amal and those above and beneath her in the archive devoted the vast majority of their time, energy, and work to the enactment of power struggles over bureaucratic positioning in the Egyptian administrative structure. The nature of the materials around which the archive existed, its entire raison d'être, was irrelevant. Bananas instead of court records could easily have been the charge of the archive. Historical research was incidental, the historian even more unimportant. What mattered most was the bureaucracy itself. The bulk of the energy and activity in the archive thus went not toward research, history, preservation, or any sense of fidelity to the sources of the past, but rather to the workings-out of authority, respect, morality, and procedure among bureaucrats; to the defense of one's position and standing in the administrative hierarchy; and to a strategy of how to operate within and advance through a complicated bureaucratic institution.

Immediately underneath Madam Amal in the bureaucratic hierarchy was Madam Mona, the perfect assistant to Madam Amal: soft-spoken, deferential, yet confident in her knowledge of the archive. Madams Amal and Mona seemed to be friends; they were about the same age and from a similar class background. They looked out for each other, knew about each other's lives, and, judging from their conversations and interactions, clearly shared a sensibility toward the world and their work. Accepting and firm in the understanding of their relative positions in the hierarchy, the two women cooperated with little evidence of competition or envy. The bureaucracy's efforts to extinguish feelings of jealousy and ambition served as a strategy to achieve efficient management and personnel function. Madam Mona knew that the only way for her to become head of the reading room—should she even desire this post—would be for Madam Amal to retire, die, or be forced out through extraordinary circumstances. Whether she expended a gargantuan or a minuscule amount of work would not change the possibilities or her opportunities.

Madam Amal and her underling acted as two hands of the same body. As I heard Madam Amal say on several occasions about their relationship—akin to Egypt and Syria during their three years together (1958 to 1961) as the United Arab Republic—"Ihna wahid" (We are one). Madam Amal trusted Madam Mona to manage the reading room as she did. It would have been foolish to try to play one off against the other, to ask Madam Mona about something that Madam Amal had already decided. No division of the archival administration was possible. If Madam Amal stepped out of the reading room, she knew her presence would be felt through Madam Mona. A third woman sometimes joined Madams Amal and Mona at the front desk, Madam Raghda; she only came to the archive one or two days a week and could often be absent for up to ten days. She wielded nowhere near the authority of Madams Amal and Mona, only carrying out simple tasks such as giving people indexes or directing them to her two seniors.

Madam Amal was physically larger and taller than Madams Mona and Raghda and was somewhat intimidating. Her forceful personality made her seem even more imposing. Her every action and word manifested her power. She sat at the head of the reading room's long front table, between researchers and their archival materials on the shelves behind her. Hers was clearly *the* position of power: the desk's first chair, closest to the door and next to the phone, a disconnected monitor, a stack of research request forms, the little plastic box where researchers put their permits when they first entered the room, various lists of research materials, a calendar, and a collection of pens. Madam Amal perched on the most comfortable chair in the room. It reclined, swiveled, and was generously padded. To her immediate left sat Madam Mona on a comparable but clearly less comfortable chair. She had very few important items in front of her—perhaps one or two pens and some research application forms. On the days she came to the archive, Madam Raghda sat to Madam Mona's left, distinctly the lowest position, on the same kind of chair that researchers used and with nothing on the desk in front of her.

When I first started working in the archive, Madam Amal was one of the few women who did not wear a veil. I took this as another sign of her unique position and of her personal strength of will in being different from the dominant world around her. About a year into my research, during that year's Ramadan, Madam Amal started to veil. Hers was a fairly simple one—none of the shiny plastic studs, intricate patterns, or flashy colors that one saw around Cairo. Her veil generally matched her outfit, usually a pantsuit. I was not sure how religious Madam Amal was. I never saw her, for example, leave the reading room to pray. My sense from talking with her and from hearing her conversations with others was that she was socially religious—that is, outwardly just religious enough to swim along unproblematically with the main flow of Egyptian society.

Two other employees inhabited the reading room, Muhammad and Radwa. As indicated by their lack of titles, they represented the bottom of the reading room's social ladder. The equivalent of bussers in a restaurant, they undertook the heavy manual labor of moving research items to and from the building's basement storage areas. As they waited in the reading room for orders from Madam Amal, Muhammad and Radwa shared the small, old, beat-up metal desk—it looked like one a sixth grader might have—that was crammed in a corner near the dusty card catalogs, far from the head table and research desks. The two of them did not fit behind that desk, in stark and purposeful contrast to the expansive wooden real estate Madam Amal and her assistants enjoyed. Madam Amal clearly relished her power over them.

Muhammad and Radwa brought research items up to the reading room around 10 or 10:30 each morning, fulfilling the requests made no later than 2:30 p.m. the day before. Madam Amal's first task each morning was to organize the previous day's requests. Those she approved—she could reject any, on any grounds, legitimate or spurious, no reason necessary—she gave to Muhammad and Radwa to fulfill, usually with special instructions; nothing was ever straightforward. For instance, Madam Amal would often direct Muhammad and Radwa to retrieve items in the order she deemed most efficient. Or she would tell them to deliver a message to someone in the storage area. Treating them as children, sometimes she explained particulars to Muhammad and Radwa that she expected they would confuse. Once she had instructed them to her satisfaction, she dispatched the two down to the storage areas with their creaking, wobbling metal pushcart. As Muhammad and Radwa made their rounds, picking up the requested materials, phone calls from various departments in the storage areas ensued. The archive's accreted numbering systems caused many misunderstandings, as bureaucrats in the basement often had to guess which numbering system had been used for a particular request, and researchers sometimes ordered items by date rather than reference number. Thus, for nearly the entire hour Muhammad and Radwa usually spent retrieving items, Madam Amal fielded calls trying to clear up the confusion of the day's requests.

When they returned to the reading room, Madam Amal always asked them, no matter how long they had been gone, "What took you so long?" Even while they were still in the basement, she often called down to different storage areas to tell them to hurry up. This daily ritual involved her scolding them for being slow and wasting time in gossiping and joking with their friends, but she usually made up for it with a joke of her own and a few smiles as Muhammad and Radwa laid out the day's haul in front of her. Captain of her ship, she inspected the catch spread out on her desk, matching request slips to registers and folders, trying to figure out what, if anything, had slipped through the net that day. Missing items were unmistakably the fault of Muhammad and Radwa—further proof of their incompetence and confirmation that they deserved their place at the bottom of the archive's hierarchy. After Madam Amal moved the day's successfully processed items to the shelves behind her, she put in more phone calls to try to clear up any outstanding requests.

One day when Muhammad worked alone—Radwa, without explanation, had not come—he fulfilled his daily tasks with his usual diligence. He unloaded the day's registers and boxes onto Madam Amal's desk, and she began her review of the materials. She found a normal smattering of mistakes. One in particular caught her attention, not because it required correction but because it offered an opportunity to further grind her authority onto Muhammad. A researcher had ordered register number 159 of the court of Rashid, a court with a few hundred registers. When Muhammad retrieved it from the basement, he read to the depot attendant the Arabic numbers on the request as English, mistaking the Arabic 159 (١٥٩) for the English 109. Confusing the Arabic symbol for five with the English symbol for zero was neither unreasonable nor uncommon, given the resemblance and the fact that researchers regularly oscillated between using Arabic and English numbers when writing requests.

Madam Amal, with register 109 on her desk, immediately pounced on Muhammad for what she saw as his stupidity and incompetence. As she made fun of him, she said, disparagingly, "Kafaya al-thaqafa bat'atak illi hatt-wadina fi siteen dahiya" (Enough of that "culture" of yours that is going to be the ruin of us all). The word for "culture," *thaqafa*, usually means high or officially sanctioned culture, what in the United States might be termed highbrow culture. The novels of Naguib Mahfouz or a Beethoven symphony are thaqafa. People who have been to university or studied abroad, journalists, poets, and famous musicians inhabit this realm. Lowbrow culture is not thaqafa. Most Egyptians do not consider singers who croon about being fruit sellers or dry cleaners (such songs exist) or writers who dwell on drinking or sex to be practitioners of thaqafa. Knowledge of English or another foreign language is one of the requisites for gaining entry into the world of thaqafa.

Therefore, when Madam Amal chided Muhammad for confusing Arabic and English numbers, she attacked his cultural and social standing, deriding his attempts to show off by pretending to know English, cementing for him his permanent exclusion from the world of thaqafa. In her view, Muhammad's pretense to culture would lead to disaster. Why? Because his striving to use English was an attempt to ascend from his strictly ascribed social class, a kind of upward cultural mobility that could only lead to bad things, as it just had, and must therefore remain impossible. Thus, Madam Amal used this incident to solidify her own station and to impress upon Muhammad her dominant position in intellect, class, and the archive's bureaucracy. He was working-class Egyptian, only knew Arabic, and therefore possessed no thaqafa; he had to content himself with his lot.

The politics of language was fraught in Egypt. Using foreign words—usually English, though at an earlier time, as Madam Amal's title attests, the same was true for French and before that Turkish—signified a certain class or personal history of education, upbringing, and travel. Many Egyptians flaunted their privilege by peppering their speech with English words and phrases. Others aspired. Fruit and juice sellers, for instance, would describe their products as "freesh." People who took over crowded street corners in Cairo to collect tips as they helped people park their cars employed technical words of their trade, such as "barking" (parking), "estob" (stop), or "kuming" (coming). Many English words related to computers entered Arabic, too. Often there were perfectly good Arabic words, but using English added cachet. It also presented risks, as Muhammad learned, since those of higher classes regularly made fun of the English used by those beneath them in the social hierarchy. A misused word, accent, or mispronunciation led to ridicule.

Growing up as the American child of Egyptian parents, I had sometimes poked fun at the way Egyptians speak English, amusing myself but annoying my parents. My mother asking where the "beers" (pears) were in the supermarket or my father ordering "Guatemala" (guacamole) in a restaurant produced many laughs. In Egypt, though, the roles reversed. Now I was the one with the accent who regularly tripped up in Arabic, the butt of my family's jokes. Just rewards for youthful insolence. In the archive, my accent coded me as clearly foreign, no matter what any official government document said. Like most bureaucrats, Madam Amal had likely taken the standard English language courses offered in Egyptian public schools, but she could not use the language in any meaningful way, such as to read a newspaper or follow a movie. Instead, she deployed English words to project expertise about what she considered technical matters—the "barinter" (printer), for example, or "el-estickare" (the sticker on the front of some registers). Registers had a "kod" (code), and every year the archive's administration released a "ribort" (report). She was also entitled to a little "rist" (rest) every now and then, just like everyone else.

Madam Amal's nemesis in the archive was a man named 'Abd al-Rahman. As the bureaucrat in charge of the basement storage areas and the release of archival materials to the reading room, he stood at near administrative parity with Madam Amal. Each ran a department, at opposite ends of the archival labor chain—he where archival materials lived, she where they were consulted. They therefore constantly communicated, as Egypt's past moved up and down between them. Because of their comparable levels of authority and their need to cooperate, power struggles shaped their every interaction. Muhammad and Radwa served as the innocent connective tissue between 'Abd al-Rahman's basement and Madam Amal's reading room. Though Madam Amal yelled at them when any of the day's requests for materials went unfulfilled, the decision to release or withhold an item lay wholly with 'Abd al-Rahman. His regular refusal to send items up from the storage areas precipitated a near ritualized cascade of decision points, phone calls, and tinder for conflict. In the case of a missing item, 'Abd al-Rahman decided how much effort to expend trying to find it. In other instances, materials proved genuinely too frail to be moved. Madam Amal reacted to every unmet request first with reflexive anger, but this response was usually quickly followed by acceptance, since fewer research materials in the reading room meant less work for her. Sometimes, though, she took 'Abd al-Rahman's refusal to release materials as a power play against her—a flexing of *his* ability to control the function of *her* reading room.

On the occasions when she chose to contest 'Abd al-Rahman—because of a particularly pushy researcher, because she knew the item had recently been used, or because she was in a mood to wrangle—their disputes subsumed the reading room. These fights raised Madam Amal's ire more than anything else. Her first move was always to call 'Abd al-Rahman to try to persuade him that this or that item should be delivered to the reading room. When these initially civil efforts failed, which they usually did, she would slam the phone down in a mini-explosion and then, yelling, explain the situation to Madam Mona. She would denounce 'Abd al-Rahman as unfair, ill-mannered, and recalcitrant. She would then strategize with Madam Mona as to how to best him in this power game. Fight fire with fire? Or not debase oneself by descending to his level? Ask Muhammad and Radwa to refuse to work with him? Report him to a higher-up? Inevitably, these conversations would digress into a critique of what kind of person 'Abd al-

Rahman was, his ethical deficiencies, and how it was so very like him to be so difficult and childish.

Because he held the authority to release or keep an item in storage, 'Abd al-Rahman delighted in these situations. On certain occasions, rather than indulge in a screaming match over the phone, he would come up to the reading room himself—unannounced—to settle matters. He sauntered into Madam Amal's domain like the mayor of his own small town and, before even looking in her direction, greeted researchers he knew. A dapper man in his mid-forties, 'Abd al-Rahman usually wore a suit and a nice watch; he was always clean-shaven, with generous amounts of product slicking his hair back. He would amble over to Madam Amal's desk, projecting an air of propriety and ease, and greet her politely, as if to indicate that he was above any petty tiffs, waving hello to Madam Mona and Madam Raghda, too, if she was there that day. He would sit in front of Madam Amal. She always stood. Her voice boomed louder than his, and she generally seemed much more agitated than he did. His coolness was part of his strategy in these interactions, as he knew it irked her. Dispute resolved or not, 'Abd al-Rahman would eventually make his exit, smiling and saying goodbye to those he had greeted on his way in. After he left, Madam Amal would continue to badmouth him, at the top of her voice, to Madam Mona.

No argument between the two ever really ended. Rather, each butting of heads simply lengthened the long line of their serial battle. In a bureaucracy in which most jobs are held for life, they knew they might work together for decades. They competed as rivals, yes, but ultimately shared interests as occupants of the same rung of the administrative hierarchy. They understood their privileges in this caste system and were aligned in their desire to defend them. This created common cause, mutual understanding, and even polite respect between them as savvy and strong-willed equals. Still, each sought to assert authority over the other. As they maneuvered, the tools available to them included invoking facets of the archive's bureaucratic strictures (as selectively enforced as they were), appeals to higher-ups in the administration, moral suasion, and the weight of social mores. Madam Amal loved to paint ʿAbd al-Rahman as morally compromised for his inconsistencies and favoritism. He chose to lean on the force of his personality to achieve his goals. Both often made recourse to their boss in the archive. The director would meet with them on occasion, never with resolution or even any noticeable change. Their relationship exemplified the machinations of relatively equal rivals in Egyptian society as they attempted to outdo each other. Ethical arguments only took one so far. Behind these cultural curtains, brute and creative power plays proved much more effective: not only the attempted application of law or the recruitment of authority, but, even more, constituency building, quid pro quo bribery, political nepotism, and corrupt careerism.

How might the lowly researcher—untrustworthy, lazy, vulnerable, nagging—operate around (or with) Madam Amal's iron authority? Avoidance proved the most successful tactic. Each day the building's fire alarm rang several short bursts to indicate that the archive's day shift—9 a.m. to 2:45 p.m.—had ended. Before she could leave, Madam Amal had to ensure that the reading room's afternoon bureaucrats had arrived. She, of course, always wanted to leave immediately, so any tardiness by the next shift angered her no end. The afternoon bureaucrats had nowhere near the power of Madam Amal. They could not accept requests for research materials, could not order items from the storage areas, and essentially did nothing but sit at the front desk of the reading room to ensure that no archival items were stolen and that researchers behaved. The archive had extended its working hours from 2:45 to around 6:30 (the exact time differed each day) not as a service to researchers but to give government workers extra hours.

In the afternoon, the desk was staffed by young men just beginning their careers on temporary contracts. Like Madam Amal and her assistants, they had not entered the archive's administration thanks to a degree in library sciences or any great interest in archival preservation; rather, their positions had come to them either through connections or through a government program that placed job applicants where there was need. They could just as easily have ended up as inspectors in meatpacking facilities or desk clerks in the railway administration. Given their limited role and lack of responsibility, they mostly spoke on the phone, joked around with each other and with researchers, sometimes played music on their cell phones or a small radio, and often left the room unattended for long stretches. Nothing sat on the desk before them. Madam Amal gleaned much of what happened in the afternoon and hated it all. She saw these young bureaucrats as troublesome and incapable. Their uselessness was further evidence that she, and only she, could maintain order and security in the reading room. She demanded that they do no harm to the regime she and the Madams built each morning—a constant worry for her because their mischievous deeds proved their fecklessness.

One afternoon, a researcher who had developed good relations with 'Abd al-Rahman and many of the staff of the basement convinced an afternoon reading room bureaucrat to allow him to call downstairs and ask one of his friends to bring up a register. This, of course, violated the archive's edifice of order and hierarchy of authority, as all requests had to be funneled through Madam Amal during the morning shift. As Egypt's traffic enforcement system proved, in highly bureaucratized structures the most logical approach for the individual is often to bypass stated protocols, as adherence to them takes more time, more money, more effort; indeed, the system itself encourages one to look for loopholes, use connections, and bribe. Given Egypt's pervasive inequality, only those with means, influence, privilege, and other resources have the ability to break rules. This researcher received his register within minutes, seeming confirmation of his connections and wiliness in working the system.

Justice came swiftly the next morning. As Madam Amal looked over the shelves, she noticed the unsanctioned register. She had not approved a request for this item, and no slip existed to evidence a request. Her temperature rose. She called down to 'Abd al-Rahman, livid, to ask how it was that a register had been allowed to come to the reading room without her permission. This was not the first incident of this sort, and Madam Amal likely knew what had happened, but she wanted 'Abd al-Rahman to admit his culpability to her. Hearing his words of confession would represent a victory in their ongoing war of attrition. Like her, he left at 2:45, but, also like her, he remained responsible for what happened in his department in the afternoon. 'Abd al-Rahman told Madam Amal he would investigate and call her back.

He phoned the reading room forty-five minutes later to inform her that he had identified the miscreant who had allowed the register to leave the basement. Was this person truly guilty? Could it have been a scapegoat, or someone against whom 'Abd al-Rahman held a vendetta? Whatever the case, Madam Amal bolted to the director's office to report the incident and, her true target, 'Abd al-Rahman, the one who had allowed this to happen. The episode confirmed everything Madam Amal already knew: researchers were conniving and could not be trusted, the afternoon bureaucrats were hopelessly incompetent, and 'Abd al-Rahman was morally bankrupt. How, indeed, could *everyone else* in the archive be so shameful and sinister? She alone stood as the archive's bulwark against evil and stupidity, and the enactment of this drama in front of all the researchers and bureaucrats in the reading room that day sent a clear message: never think you can outsmart Madam Amal. Correcting the wrong by returning the register to the storage area, punishing the deceitful researcher, and making clear to all the injury 'Abd al-Rahman had caused, Madam Amal restored order and reasserted the unshakability of her authority.

Some researchers planned their entire schedule around the presence and absence of Madam Amal. Those who actively avoided her often did so after an argument or some other negative interaction. Many more, as one of my friends explained, preferred to work in the afternoon because the reading room was much calmer and more lax without Madam Amal's constant conversations, loud phone calls, barking of orders, and generally domineering presence. My friend loathed Madam Amal's *manzara*, a term derived from a family of words related to seeing, viewing, and authority that means something like showing off or demonstrating one's dominance. Madam Amal loved to practice this public puffing of power for all to see and hear.

She determined not only the when of research but also the what. If Madam Amal disliked a researcher for any reason, she could easily withhold materials from him. By the same token, she could make the lives of researchers she liked not only more pleasant but also more productive. Because so much of the writing of history depends on seeing original sources— the discovery of new materials often completely reshapes a field's historiography—our priestess's ultimate authority to bestow or deny shaped the writing of Egyptian history in real and significant ways. A colleague of mine had been working on

the history of education in late nineteenth-century Egypt for
about a year before Madam Amal mentioned to him, in passing, a very obviously useful archival unit related to the history
of schooling. Without an index or catalog, he had no way of
knowing this set of sources existed. Had Madam Amal chosen
not to tell him about it, he likely never would have known
about documents that ultimately figured prominently in his
work. This chance comment by Madam Amal—a bureaucrat
with no formal training in history or archival sciences—motivated by some unknown force, in the end radically affected
my colleague's scholarship and, once his work was published,
the world's knowledge of Egypt's past. Why on that day, after
hundreds of days in which this historian had worked in the
archive, did Madam Amal choose to divulge this secret information? Chance, luck, whim, and Madam Amal's mood thus
proved some of the arbitrary forces that determined the writing
of Egyptian history. We must grapple with this reality: Egyptian history written during Madam Amal's tenure depended
on her actions, temperament, and feelings toward particular
researchers. She shaped Egypt's past and historians' futures.

In the archive's hierarchy, where inequality reigned, I devoted far too much time to contemplating means of maneuvering in Madam Amal's world of absolute power. After a year
of near-daily interactions with her, I had successfully proved
myself a trustworthy researcher who would not steal documents. I had built up a certain amount of capital with her—
limited capital that I knew I had to manage carefully—which
won me certain privileges. I could now, for example, phone
in orders for materials instead of having to come in and write
them myself. I gained nothing more than any other researcher
had who came in on a regular basis, and I was thankful for
everything. Our relationship had settled into a comfortable
rhythm of friendliness. No matter the rapport we had estab-

lished, I—of course—understood that Madam Amal was still and forever in charge.

My point of decision came out of a conversation with one of my aunts during our regular Friday lunch. She asked me how my research was progressing, and I explained that both my work with my sources and my relationship with Madam Amal seemed to be in a good place. She suggested that a gift to Madam Amal might help to move things along even more, and the idea she seeded grew in my head for a few months. I understood Egypt well enough to know that gift-giving worked as a social lubricant, and I had read several histories and anthropologies of gifting in graduate school; Marcel Mauss's essay was a favorite. Given the politics of the archive, though, I was unsure how a gift would play with Madam Amal. I knew nothing would change my station in the hierarchy, and I did not want to rock the boat given the modest status I had achieved. I proceeded carefully.

I appreciated Madam Amal. She had authorized and facilitated the research that would form the core of my dissertation and professional career. That seemed more than worthy of a gift, so why not express my gratitude? I wanted to thank her but did not want her to wonder if I was proffering a bribe or, even worse, to think I thought she was bribable. Offending a person who held unqualified power over me would, obviously, be wholly detrimental. I had to avoid giving the impression that I expected privileges in the archive (I did not) because I was a wealthy foreigner (I was not). But then again, truth be told, if a gift could help my situation, I was not going to be unhappy about it. Maybe Madam Amal expected a gift from me precisely *because* I was a foreigner. I knew that other researchers, both Egyptian and non-Egyptian, had given her gifts in the past. If I did give her something, I would not want anyone to know—to think that I was trying to bribe Madam Amal or curry favor with her. Was I tying myself up in knots because I was an American who believed in some fantasy of merit or equality? Was I legitimating the Egyptian stereotype of the cheap American? If I did not give her a gift, would this hurt my future work in the archive? In my mind, fine lines separated the perception of a gift as a sincere gesture, a bribe, or an expected decorum. And what would I even get her? Something practical? Decorative? Sweet? Something for her two young daughters?

To break through the confusion my aunt's suggestion had precipitated, I turned to one of my closer friends in the archive, a historian named Mustafa, who had given Madam Amal gifts in the past. Mustafa assured me that a gift, if offered discreetly and humbly, could only help and surely not hurt. He explained to me how best to go about it. Call Madam Amal the day before, mostly to confirm that she would be there the next day. Then arrive very early in the morning, soon after Madam Amal and well before her assistants and most researchers. Present the gift to her, describing it as just a small expression of thanks for all she had done over the course of my research. Add that I hoped she liked it. Leave without working that day. When I asked Mustafa what I should get her, he suggested something for the house.

I ended up giving Madam Amal two gifts over the course of my years in the archive: a box of nice chocolates on Ramadan and a serving platter before I left for a research trip to Turkey. Both occasions went smoothly, I'm thankful to say. I followed Mustafa's advice to the letter. I called the day before. When I arrived, we exchanged pleasantries, no real conversation, but a genuine moment of connection. She knew why I was there, I offered up my token of gratitude, and she thanked me. Her eyes twinkled, which warmed me. I left, and not a word passed about the gifts after that. I never determined whether

Madam Amal liked them or if they helped or hurt my life in the archive. I had no major problems going forward, but I had no way of knowing if this had anything to do with the gifts or not. I chose to believe that she appreciated them and that they brought us closer. As with everything in the reading room, Madam Amal held the secret tight.

5
Volume

In physics, noise refers to irregular fluctuations in data that lie outside the normal range of a signal or other phenomenon. They are additions, disturbances, exceptions, distractions that hinder the transfer of information or sully an otherwise clean dataset and therefore should be removed or ignored. Historians generally treat the ubiquitous audible noise of the archive in the same way—as an accepted and expected aspect of research to tolerate and ignore, a meaningless annoyance of the craft. As in physics, we learn to tune it out, not to allow it to distract us from the main thrust of our research. What, though, if we took this noise seriously, as a constituent part of historical practice rather than a challenge to it? How might we historians account for noise? If, indeed, as in the Egyptian National Archives, it is everywhere, how does it figure into the scholarship produced in and from a particular archive? Outside of the archive, across Egypt in the 2000s, had one listened closely enough, he or she would have heard voices declaring grievance and injury. Given that noise proves so fundamental to the everyday lived experience of both doing history and being in history, surely it must affect the writing of history. Could one write a historical narrative that accounts for, instead of always ignoring, archival noise? Where, in fact, does the ever dominant noise of the archive go? Could we write it in, integrate it? The quiet notes lying in repose at the end of our books offer no direction here.

We must listen for the noise. We must listen to the noise. For many historians, the exceptions, outliers, or anomalies usually disregarded in dominant historical narratives offer the chance to challenge those narratives by pointing to their flaws and blind spots. By allowing in the long marginalized, these histories have sketched a more fulsome, polyvocal, and accurate picture of the past than those that consider only the majority view. Standing on a data point far distant from the main curve of historical scholarship, focusing on peoples, events, and phenomena that have been ignored, taking seriously the traditionally eschewed noise of the archive offers a far more complete rendering of the historian's craft and a chance to hear the whispers of other histories. We historians are not simply receivers of signals sent out by pulsating archival documents. We should not surround ourselves with noise-deadening mental foam to try to silence everything but the pure transfer of information from paper to historian. So much more occurs as we read our sources.

Indeed, the vast majority of what occurs in the reading room is *not* the quiet reflection of historians reading documents. History is done as it is made, in the presence of others, in a living, breathing, messy, loud world where personalities clash, mobile phones ring, stomachs rumble, guns fire, and minds wander. Why not write this history? Why not focus on the preponderant experience of doing history? Why not paint the more complete picture of how our citations came to be, one that includes instead of dismisses the outlying noisy data? We lose something in the silence. The traditional cleaned-up narratives of past events and phenomena that we imbibe from historical scholarship are partial; they exclude an enormous swath of experience, interaction, and thought. Let us turn up the volume on the noise of the archival experience, then, and, for the moment, strip away the normal mainstays of staid historical writing.

Noise in the Egyptian National Archives ranged in form, timbre, and tenor. The indomitable Madam Amal practiced a politics of speech in the reading room that projected and solidified her iron authority. More than anyone else, she spoke in the archive. And when she spoke, you heard, even if you didn't listen. She raised her voice on the phone, when conversing with Madams Mona and Raghda, when talking to researchers, and when giving orders to Muhammad and Radwa. Her fights with 'Abd al-Rahman, both in person and over the phone, were broadcast live for the entire reading room. Her power derived in part from the fact that she made no effort to lower her voice, whereas everyone else had to. Madam Amal's monopoly of projection accomplished two tasks. It relayed information—the archive will close early tomorrow, the basement staff have lost the day's request slips, do not trifle with me today—and, more significantly, trumpeted her authority in the reading room. Her booming voice and the cadence of her speech constituted its inescapable soundtrack.

Because the reading room offered one of the more comfortable spaces in the archive complex—it was, unlike most areas, air conditioned, had plenty of chairs, and was conveniently situated next to the café—it functioned as a kind of piazza for bureaucrats, who constantly streamed in and out to chat and gossip with Madam Amal and to say hello to Madams Mona and Raghda and sometimes even to Muhammad and

Radwa too. Madam Amal held forth in these assemblies. Her gregarious personality attracted others, and her quick-wittedness manifested in a strong opinion no matter the topic. Madam Amal knew how to engage others and to use her skills as raconteur to cultivate her prestige in the archive's bureaucracy. Faced with the reality of a paltry government salary for her difficult work, Madam Amal derived self-esteem from the respect she earned by galvanizing her peers and underlings through her speech acts. For example, when a new employee entered the reading room for the first time, Madam Amal made a point of having an independent conversation with that person. She would announce for all to hear that she needed to have a word and then would take the fresh bureaucrat aside or even outside the reading room. By making public her wish to speak to this person in private, Madam Amal created an aura of curiosity around the mystery of this conversation. She cornered individuals both to intimidate them and to make them feel special, by tasking them with a particular job or role in her universe of interests and prestige. Succeed in this freighted first test and much would be won. Hers was a perfected brand of bureaucratic performance art.

More than just Madam Amal's decibels reverberated through the reading room. At any given time, multiple conversations might be running among researchers, too. The archive was ultimately a friendly place where most everyone knew most everyone else. New faces immediately gained notice and demanded conversation, especially foreigners and in particular Egyptian American anomalies like me. When I first arrived, my fellow researchers welcomed me warmly and always proved very friendly. We drank tea together and exchanged all sorts of research suggestions. People would often come to my desk just to say hello, share something they found, or ask about books. I would do the same. Some of my closest friendships emerged from these conversations. Quite often, people sitting at neighboring desks chatted as they transcribed, or a group gathered around a single desk to talk. All of the reading room's conversations—the extremely pleasant ones I had, the ones I overheard—laid down a regular, sometimes welcome, sometimes disruptive tempo to archival work.

Political speech—politics generally—was dangerous in Egypt. If one was not a member of Mubarak's ruling National Democratic Party, one was by definition oppositional and therefore liable to lose a job, face intimidation or imprisonment, or even be killed. Only bad came from politics and so most Egyptians shied away from discussing it, let alone engaging in it. Whispers, though, could become roars. In the three decades before 2011, the government had purposefully and mostly successfully depoliticized the country, diverting the populace's energy and attention toward culture, sports, consumerism, movies, television, fashion, truly anything other than its political past, present, or future. This politics of the depolitical played out audibly in the archive every day.

A continuous string of causes célèbres busied the Egyptian public. The latest scandals sat just below headlines about what Mubarak had done that day. The state proudly announced its corruption and then distracted from it. Fodder for one of the more spirited conversations in the reading room came from a particularly sensationalized episode of a popular television program called *The Hala Show*. Hosted by a woman named Hala Sarhan, this nightly broadcast was akin to *Oprah* or *Ellen* in the United States. One night Hala welcomed a group of sex workers to tell of their trade, their lives, and their clients. This episode was massively hyped, hence highly anticipated and widely watched. I tuned in. The show took pains to conceal the identities of the women and their clients, blurring their faces and altering their voices. A few days after it aired, problems began. One of the women gave an interview to a newspaper claiming that none of the women featured were actually sex workers but had been paid by *The Hala Show* to play the part. Hala had hidden their identities not to protect them but to cover up the fact that they were actors. The woman went on to assert that the show had in fact not adequately disguised their faces or voices, since the women's husbands and families recognized them. With their identities revealed, all of the women claimed to be actors, but their families either did not believe them or found the shame overwhelming. The husband of one woman divorced her, and myriad other harms befell them and their families. Soon there were calls in the press and elsewhere for Hala to be held accountable. Threatened with lawsuits and even physical violence, Hala fled the country, first to Dubai and then to London.

Such soap-opera scandals involving celebrities, secrets, sex, and lies are, of course, regular features of our media-saturated lives, and they are as momentarily gripping in Egypt as they are elsewhere. For Madams Amal and Mona and others in the archive, "the Hala incident" generated wide-ranging discussion. As the story unfolded over a period of two weeks or so, the staff and numerous researchers reviewed and analyzed its every turn from every possible angle. Were the women actors pretending to be sex workers or sex workers pretending to be actors? Was Hala ultimately responsible, or should these women—whether actors or sex workers—have known better? Perhaps Hala lied, but she did pay the women. Did the women lie? Maybe the directors of the show duped Hala. Should one expect truth from television? Scrutiny and debate abounded. Madam Amal and I thought it was all a stunt, fabrications aimed at ratings. We bonded over this agreement, united against those who thought Hala was the target of a smear campaign. To socialize in these weeks, one had to have an opinion. Every day in the archive, hours of discussion colonized our brains—the latest developments, arguments for and against, how it would end. As our eyes read of the past, our ears filled with tales of the Egyptian present.

If the politics of the depolitical succeeded in distracting the Egyptian public with social spectacle, it failed utterly to provide economically. A state that excelled in policing so much of life could not support its citizenry with basic goods and services. Cavernous wealth gaps meant that a tiny sliver of friends of the state gained enormous riches while the majority barely subsisted. Employees in the archive, as across Egypt's bureaucracy, did not earn a living wage. To overcome these economic impossibilities, informal networks filled the void, providing people with cheaper food and cheaper shelter, a second job and basic health care. One such network operated in the archive. Every week, on Tuesday or Wednesday morning, a woman who worked in another section stopped by the reading room with two or three garbage bags of children's clothing. Alongside her government job, she ran a small business buying cheap and good-quality children's clothing from a wholesaler to resell. She took orders and could usually deliver within a month. On the mornings she came to the reading room, all work ceased for half an hour or so as Madam Amal and her staff laid out girls' jeans and tops, boys' shirts and sweaters, on their expansive desk, all the while discussing sizes and styles, what they liked and didn't like, reviewing previous orders, and putting in new ones. Madam Amal would inquire, for example, whether a pair of gloves on offer was *gild* (leather) or, more desirable and couched in the technical language of English, "estretch." The whole business was always boisterous, with laughter and buoyant chatter greasing the wheels.

With their backs to the room, Madams Amal and Mona forgot about court records and ministry reports, concentrat-

ing fully on the onesies before them. We researchers knew not
to interrupt them as they haggled in this pop-up marketplace.
Understandably, they cared more about this commerce than
about archival materials. On the razor-thin margins of their
salaries, saving a few pounds here and there could be the dif-
ference between a lean month and a comfortable one. In these
moments of distracted shopping, the unremitting obsession
with security fell away. Although calamity never struck, what
would have transpired if a theft occurred because of Madam
Amal's inattention during one of her purchasing sessions? Or
what if the director of the archive had come in while his employees were buying and selling boys' socks? Would he close
down the black-market business? I guessed he would not, since
this trade helped to keep his employees afloat in a world where
their salaries, he knew, did not. Such resourceful informal networks within Egypt's inefficient bureaucratic institutions alle-
viated some of the failures of the state in serving people's vital
needs. As Egyptians did what they could to sustain themselves,
a desk became a store, a closet a restaurant, and an archival
reading room a noisy marketplace.

More than the weekly shopping, pop culture commentary,
or Madam Amal's incessant bickering with 'Abd al-Rahman, the
cell phone represented the greatest source of noise in the reading room. Egyptians love their cell phones. Everyone has one,
indeed must have one. Some have more than one. Even the
homeless have cell phones. Often people carry a charger, too,
as they regularly exhaust the battery over the course of a day.
Around 2004, phone technology in Egypt was more advanced
than in the United States. Because its mobile network more
closely matched the global system, Egypt received the latest
models from Japan, Korea, and China as soon as they were released. Varieties and options proved endless. More than almost
any other physical object, the cell phone shaped life in Egypt.

Although they were prohibited in the reading room, nearly every second, it seemed, a cell phone rang or pinged with a message. Because every researcher and every bureaucrat had a phone (and a few had two), there were anywhere from fifteen to thirty mobile phones in the reading room at any given time. Ringtones were set to pop songs, Quranic recitations, a child's voice, and all kinds of chimes and beeps (vibrate and silence existed as options too, of course, but were rarely used). Cell phones exercised a destabilizing and depoliticizing politics of interruption that, like the government of Egypt in the 2000s, provided little space for reflection, solitude, or escape. Relentless noise—a then-popular Nancy 'Agram song or Surat Yusuf—disciplined communicative forms of interaction.

In Egypt, people nearly always answered their phones. Receiving a call was free but making one was not, so there was a strong incentive to answer. Voicemail cost extra and was therefore seldom added to a mobile plan. When a phone rang, the owner generally answered as quickly as possible, before the caller hung up. Of course, sometimes people did let their phones ring a few times as they deliberated—despite the potential costs of a call back—whether or not they wanted to answer. Not answering a call was a rare event that usually prompted worry that someone was injured or in trouble, and, therefore, more calls ensued to check. Once, when I was attending a large academic conference featuring some of Egypt's most prominent historians and intellectuals, the cell phone of the highly respected scholar giving the keynote lecture rang. The microphone amplified it through the speakers, filling the room with reverb. Without skipping a beat, he pulled the phone from his inside jacket pocket, looked to see who was calling, and proceeded to answer. He conducted an admittedly short conversation, returned the phone to his pocket, and continued his lecture as if nothing had happened. We the audience of a few hundred sat in polite silence throughout, taking the call in stride as a non-event.

Mobile phones proved a key realm in which Madam Amal practiced the politics of speech and further flexed her authority. Despite the prohibition against phone usage in the reading room, Madam Amal, naturally, reserved for herself the right to talk on her cell phone and the archive's internal phone as much and as loudly as she wanted. Indeed, she spent much of her day on the phone, engaged predominantly in conversations of a personal or family nature. When a call came in on her cell phone, she usually did not answer immediately but checked the caller and then let it ring a few more times. Her phone was never set to vibrate or silent. All of this served further notice that the rules did not apply to Madam Amal. She could make all the noise she wanted. She further impressed her prestige on the reading room by advertising her monopoly of the archive's internal phone, which only she could use. Here she loudly discharged the affairs of the reading room: requesting materials, looking for Muhammad and Radwa, or calling other departments. Because Madam Amal knew many people throughout the archive and because problems were often complex—and, in truth, out of sheer boredom—she spent hours on the internal phone, untangling bureaucratic knots and also asking about people's families, catching up, and gossiping. The phone extended the reach of the reading room as the archive's public square and Madam Amal's central orchestrating role within it. She never lowered her voice, projecting her conversations and authority in high fidelity. Her daughters sometimes called her on the internal phone. Her loving and tender tone with them cut a pleasant contrast to her normal commanding tenor.

As part of the exercise of her power, Madam Amal selectively—even arbitrarily, it seemed at times—berated those who used their phones in the reading room. Researchers usually took calls at their desks while they continued to read their materials. Only if a call extended did researchers—but never staff—leave the reading room of their own volition. The chief criterion determining Madam Amal's choice of whom to chastise seemed to be the individual's place in the social hierarchy. She targeted only the lowliest. One day, the cell phone of a young male researcher rang with a loud and obnoxious ringtone. This young man came to the archive every day, working diligently on a master's thesis; he was friendly and seemed to know many of the other researchers. He answered, as most everyone did, and a conversation started. As he was a young student from a provincial university with no important title or position (he was not even a doctoral student), Madam Amal shouted at him from across the room that talking on mobile phones was not allowed. Continuing his conversation, he acknowledged her without making eye contact, only raising his hand (a gesture she did not appreciate) as he got up from his desk and left the reading room.

When he returned and passed Madam Amal's desk, she stopped him with a scowl and fired off a moral rebuke. When he first came to the archive, she began, he had worked properly, without distraction, and did not talk too much with other researchers or on his phone. Lately, though, he had started to talk a lot and did not work as conscientiously as before. What happened to you, she probed without asking. Why this fall? Like a mother scolding her child, she aimed to shame the man by making a public example of him for behavior that was technically prohibited but largely tolerated. Many times before, perhaps even most times before, Madam Amal had said nothing when the phone of a student of the same stature rang in the reading room. Why target him? Why today? The arbitrariness of this pillorying advanced Madam Amal's overall strategy of rule, a junior version of a wider Egyptian politics. Everyone had to remain always vigilant. Judgment—like the ring of a phone—could come at any moment. Key, too, as before, was the publicness of the shaming; all must obediently conform to the strictures of Madam Amal.

Fifteen minutes later, the cell phone of one of the most respected professors in Egypt pierced the room just a few desks away from the student whom Madam Amal had reprimanded. The professor answered her phone, had a conversation, and then returned to work. Neither Madam Amal nor anyone else even looked up; we all simply kept working. The professor herself clearly never even whiffed the thought of ignoring or silencing her phone, speaking softly, or leaving the room. No one, of course, complained of a double standard. We accepted the premise, as normal as the air we breathed, that this professor enjoyed—nay, *deserved*—sundry privileges: ordering as many registers as she wanted and receiving them immediately, using a pen, photocopying, even drinking tea in the reading room, and, of course, using her phone as she liked. Certain people in Egypt *were* above the law. This was as true in the archive as outside it. The older, well established, and well connected received luxuries and advantages that were not only denied others but were against theoretical rules.

The problem of noise in the archive revealed other layers in the stratigraphy of class, distinction, and authority in Egypt. One day in late winter, a Swiss researcher named Laura sat with her computer at a desk in front of an Egyptian researcher named Rasha. Although laptops were permitted in the reading room, most Egyptian researchers could not afford them, so those using them tended to be foreigners. Rasha was a portly lady in her mid-forties. Her clothes, jewelry, and phone suggested money. She was married with three children and, I learned through conversations with her, had decided to start on a graduate degree later than most. This made her unique among the archive's researchers. Her doctoral dissertation tackled the history of Alexandria during the period of Ottoman rule. Rasha was one of the loudest researchers in the reading room, talking on the phone incessantly, usually to her children, to the point that she wore a headset with a microphone jutting out from underneath her veil so that she could speak hands-free while thumbing through her registers. Phone charges clearly did not concern Rasha. Because she was an older woman who had worked in the archive for many years and usually sat in the back row, Madam Amal tended to leave her alone.

Rasha was pleasant and amicable, liked by most people. Laura, on the other hand, was not. Women in Egypt—foreigners and citizens alike—have to be constantly on the defensive against the lascivious eyes of Egyptian men and their inappropriate behavior. Egypt is a notorious world leader in sexual harassment. Like many women in Egypt, Laura had understandably, perhaps even necessarily, developed a rough, standoffish public face. Egyptian men in the archive remain Egyptian men, so Laura proved reticent with them and with many women too. She was always polite but was short with most people, and she did not expend any energy on making friends or small talk. Since conversation was an important social lubricant that helped one to navigate the archive—getting hints from other researchers, learning about different archival units, seeking guidance in reading difficult passages—Laura's completely logical attitude both hindered her research and alienated many. Indeed, she seemed to confirm the Egyptian opinion of most foreigners: arrogant, cold, mean, aloof, unfriendly. Added to this were rumors that Laura was Jewish—never a help to one's cause in post-1948 Egypt.

One day, Rasha interrupted Laura's typing to ask her to type more quietly since the noise of the keystrokes was disturbing her. In a place where phones rang nearly every minute and groups of people regularly carried on lively conversations—and given that this comment came from a woman who talked on her phone perhaps more than any other researcher in the archive—Laura, who rarely spoke to anyone, took Rasha's request as more than rich: at best, an unreasonable request; at worst, a provocation. She turned around in her chair and told Rasha in a respectful but firm voice that there was nothing loud about her typing, that she would continue with her work, and that the real noise in the reading room was coming from her and other researchers. If Rasha really cared about noise, Laura added, she should stop talking on her phone and ask other researchers to do the same.

This set Rasha aflame. Here she was, a respectable forty-something mother of three, with money, who had worked in the archive for years, being told off by a younger, foreign, possibly Jewish researcher who had spent only a few months in the archive and in that time done little to earn any social capital. For Rasha, class and status mattered more than any honest assessment of the situation. For Laura, the opposite was true. Rasha lifted her large frame from her chair and stormed to the front of the room, muttering to herself. When she reached Madam Amal's desk (she, of course, had witnessed the whole scene), she implored her to do something. For whatever reason—either because Laura was right (computers are allowed in the reading room, she was not typing loudly, Rasha does talk on the phone excessively) or because it served Madam Amal's strategic interests to cut Rasha down a bit—she refused to intervene, telling Rasha that Laura had done nothing wrong. This infuriated Rasha even more. Archival cacophony crescendoed to crisis. Not only had Rasha been snubbed by Laura, but her appeal to the highest authority in the reading room had been rejected. Even more injurious to Rasha's pride, Madam Amal seemed to be taking Laura's side.

With her options in the reading room exhausted, Rasha took her case straight to the top—to the director of the archive. In the universe of the archive, Madam Amal stood above Rasha—a student, after all—but outside the bureaucratic hierarchy, Rasha, a woman of means, clearly bested Madam Amal. Now the two hierarchies clashed. Rasha returned from the director's office visibly pleased with herself and announced loudly, for all to hear, that the director wanted to see both herself and Madam Amal in his office. The public staging of this spectacle represented a declaration of war. Rasha had, I heard later, complained to the director that the reading room was very noisy (true in no small measure thanks to her) and that Madam Amal did nothing to enforce any semblance of quiet (also mostly true). The director of the archive would never have entertained such a complaint from, or even have met with, any of the other students working in the reading room. Not the truth of the matter but Rasha's clothes, age, class, and bearing won her his attention.

One outcome of the director's meeting with Madam Amal and Rasha was the appearance the next day of several handwritten signs headed "Rules of the Reading Room" taped to the walls. These placards dictated that, among other things, mobile phones were prohibited, conversation had to be kept to a minimum and conducted in a low voice, no two researchers could sit at the same desk, only pencils were allowed, and, above all, the quiet nature of the reading room had to be respected. This was a coup. With a speed heretofore unseen in the archive, a publicly displayed list of rules had appeared, aimed at ensuring that this place of research would be quiet and well ordered.

It remained for Madam Amal to reassert her dominance. A few days after the incident, Rasha was transcribing a document with a pen (a violation of the newly posted strictures) when her phone rang with its usual sonorousness. Before the first ring ended Madam Amal jolted straight up and walked to Rasha's desk at the back of the room, faster than I had ever seen her move before. Without saying a word, she snatched the pen out of Rasha's hand and stomped away. The two women spent the rest of the day glowering and growling at each other. Even so, the grudge dissipated quickly. Madam Amal knew she would be seeing Rasha almost daily, and constant vigilance and enforcement required more effort than letting things slide. As she did with regard to 'Abd al-Rahman, once Madam Amal had successfully reestablished her clout, she allowed the reading room to revert to its status quo ante.

The implementation of the "Rules of the Reading Room" lasted about a week. Although the placards remained on the wall, the archive returned to its ringing, clanking, chatty normal. The signs, in fact, seemed to mock what the reading room actually was with what it was supposed to be.

6

Issues

In 2004, Ahmed caught a master's student from Cairo University attempting to steal the pages of a seventeenth-century *waqf*. A waqf is a financial instrument in Islamic law that allows one to endow the proceeds of a property or other asset for a charitable or familial purpose. Like archival documents, they are meant to exist in perpetuity. After Ahmed found the documents tucked between the student's papers as he was leaving the building, the director ordered the archive closed for an indefinite period to determine how this crime could have occurred, to come up with a procedure to prevent it from ever happening again, and to train the staff in new protocols.

Had the student been commissioned to steal the waqf pages, or did he do so of his own volition, hoping to sell them later? Families often relied on such documents in suits they brought against the government to reclaim waqf properties that had been seized from them. Perhaps he had been hired by a family to these ends. Or maybe he stole the waqf not for money but to prevent other historians from seeing it. Whatever his reason, his crime forever banned him from the archive and expelled him from Cairo University. Well deserved, I thought. This student's stupidity closed the archive, and there was no telling when it would open again. It stood shuttered to us researchers; those who mattered most, the archive's staff, continued to go to work every day. Why did the feckless actions of one person translate to collective punishment? Eventually, two long weeks after the incident, the archive reopened to researchers.

A new regime of order and security had taken hold. The procedures and protocols that had previously been drizzled over everything now soaked all the way through. Ahmed personally signed every book, notebook, or loose piece of paper brought into the archive. Certifying what entered regulated what left. Any materials exiting the archive without Ahmed's signature were assumed to be stolen. The overall aim of this formerly ignored, newly reinvigorated, highly cumbersome procedure was to press researchers to bring only the bare minimum into the building. Books, bags, and other personal effects were to be kept in the dedicated storage area away from the reading room. Before the theft, one could bypass the storage room and carry personal belongings into the reading room, simply leaving them at the front near Madam Amal's desk. Now, we were allowed only a few sheets of loose paper—nothing bound—and a pencil. Laptops were acceptable but received special scrutiny.

The edifice of her dominion shaken by a theft from her domain, Madam Amal responded to the challenge as she always did—by reasserting her authority through overwhelming force. She impressed upon all of us that the world had fundamentally changed. Scolding us like children, she told us that we had brought this on ourselves. We had been given privileges and shown ourselves unworthy of them; we had only our failings to thank for our punishments. Even more than before, every researcher entered the archive first and foremost as a potential criminal. The theft had borne out the logic of this supposition. The thief was one of us, so all of us were suspect. Madam Amal smiled even less, stood much more, and roamed among the desks, lording over us like a tigress. Needless to say, this made the lives of researchers much more unpleasant.

Madam Amal inspected everyone who entered the reading room, on the lookout for a book or a bound notebook, and made sure that every loose sheet of paper carried Ahmed's signature. She and her staff now counted the number of pages in every register and every box when the item was given to a researcher and again when it was returned. If they found any discrepancy, they would assume the researcher had stolen something. This proved far from an exact science, and the arduous process markedly increased Madam Amal's workload. Registers regularly contained more than two hundred pages and boxes could hold all sorts of documents, pamphlets, and newspaper clippings. It was easy to count two pages as one, skip over a page, or miss a small piece of paper tucked away in a pamphlet. Was a newspaper clipping glued to another sheet of paper one document or two? Should an empty page in a register be counted?

Some boxes and registers had their total number of pages written on the outside already, thanks to a previous count. Madam Amal and her assistants always recounted. What if the new count differed from the number on the outside—which number was to be taken as true? Answers to these sorts of questions proved crucial, since any discrepancies would be assumed to be evidence of a theft, triggering a lengthy investigation and, no matter the result, a chain of negative consequences for the researcher involved and endless labor for the archive's staff. What if the whole kerfuffle was based on a miscount? That was unthinkable; Madam Amal never miscounted. After about two weeks, this system of counting pages ended. It was simply too much work. However, Madam Amal and her staff continued to examine every researcher's materials on the way out. Inspections now occurred three times as one left the archive: by Madam Amal in the reading room, by the worker staffing the storage area, and by Ahmed at the front security desk.

Within the logic of this renewed security regime, even those of us who had been working in the archive on a nearly daily basis for years, and whom Madam Amal knew well, became accomplices in a sudden elaborate conspiracy of archival grand larceny. Researchers had broken a sacred trust, not only with the archive as an institution but with Madam Amal personally. She had allowed us access to the hallowed history of Egypt and we had broken our covenant. She regarded us with disdain, blamed us collectively, and hence would punish us collectively. Her mindset and actions mirrored the Egyptian state's view of its citizens. The government gives, the people take. The state doles out gifts and patronage. It builds roads and tunnels, provides jobs, and defends Egypt's borders. The citizenry mostly avoids paying taxes, regularly skips out on government jobs, and complains. As the state sees it, Egyptians are greedy and ungrateful moochers, thieves who take what is not theirs: the infrastructure, security, and money the state has created. They are not to be trusted and require constant policing and often punishment. Ultimately a representative of the state, Madam Amal embodied the state's violent paternalism through her own brand of archival maternalism. In her kinship construction, young males proved especially suspicious. Madam Amal had two daughters and was fond of saying— jokingly and not—that she did not like boys. She watched male researchers more intensely and searched their belongings more thoroughly.

As was commonplace in Egypt, and as always happened in the archive, despite the enormous energy and care exercised immediately after a security breach, vigilance dissipated quickly and things eventually returned to their relatively lax pre-theft rhythms. This had happened with the "Rules of the Reading Room" that were plastered up after the Rasha incident, and it happened again now. Not only did Madam Amal and her staff quickly stop counting pages, but very soon pens returned, and gradually notebooks and other bound items as well. The general feeling of suspicion that had gripped us all slowly faded away.

Then, about two years later, confirming everything Madam Amal knew to be true of historians, another egregious heist attempt was thwarted. A doctoral candidate from a southern Egyptian university (cosmopolitan Cairenes generally maligned southerners as stupid, uncultured, conniving, and uncouth) was apprehended trying to steal about thirty documents from a box. I was in the reading room on the day of the crime, but, evidently like everyone else, did not notice anything out of the ordinary until Madam Amal received a call from Ahmed, downstairs, who had found the documents secreted among other papers stuffed into a plastic folder (plastic folders—my favorite were those with "My Clear Bag" embossed on them—had been allowed back in again). How could such a large cache of documents have been so easily smuggled out of the reading room? The culprit was caught at the last possible moment before he left the building. The practice of triple-checking personal belongings had been given up fairly quickly after the previous theft; now only Ahmed checked.

When Ahmed informed Madam Amal of his discovery,

she started yelling over the phone and also to her assistants. At first we did not know what the uproar was about, but clearly something big was happening and we soon gathered that the commotion would suck us all in, whether as unwitting parties to a crime or, more simply, as spectators of the theater that was about to play out. Research, it was obvious now, would be set aside for the day. Madam Amal roared at Madam Mona to take the box the student had been reading off the shelf. It was one of those that had the total number of pages written on the outside. Madam Amal counted the contents, and, indeed, thirty pages were missing. She bolted out of the reading room, straight to the director's office, and the two of them proceeded downstairs to Ahmed's security desk. I heard about the scene later. A burly government employee held the thief by the collar, and, for added protection and intimidation, a few other imposing men surrounded the pair. When Madam Amal reached the desk, she immediately seized the pilfered pages—*her* pages. The director made several phone calls, and the police arrived to haul the student away.

In the half hour between the time Madam Amal left the reading room and returned with the thirty stolen pages, we researchers had congregated around her desk—our public square—to figure out what was happening. We plied the other Madams with questions and discussed the man who had stolen the documents. He had not been working in the archive for long and no one knew much about him. When Madam Amal reappeared, like a heroic soldier returning from enemy lands having redeemed a captive, she strutted toward us, almost in slow motion, with her unique ability to express both confidence and disgust in the same look. She handed the retrieved pages to Madam Mona to return to the box. She then proceeded to narrate the downstairs events. We gathered around her like a kindergarten class at story time.

The plotline she set forth, of her own heroism, served to reinforce her status in the prestige culture of the reading room. With her characteristic flair, she regaled us with equal parts drama and detail. Making plain her disappointment in us, she doubled down on the assertion that we, the criminally predisposed historians, were all culpable. After all she had done for us—her sacrifice and devotion—how could we have betrayed her like this yet again? Distancing herself from any blame, she held us researchers alone responsible for the student's vile act. Once more, we would be forced to change our behavior, to ensure that nothing like this ever happened again.

In the next few days, Madam Amal and the director devoted themselves to ascertaining how the theft had come to pass; in doing this they did everything they could to shore up Madam Amal's position of authority. She could not be perceived to be at fault in any way. The historical narrative that Madam Amal had begun to construct the moment she arrived back in the reading room, which was settled upon as truth, was that the student had purloined the documents while Madam Amal was in the basement storage area, having been called there to deal with 'Abd al-Rahman's ineptitude. He could not find some documents she had called up and so, typically, she herself had to go downstairs to clear up the matter. While she was gone, the reading room was in the hands of her assistants, and this is when the theft had occurred. The student clearly would never have dared to do such a thing while Madam Amal was in the room. According to this account, the theft was therefore the fault of every archive employee *except* Madam Amal—'Abd al-Rahman for his inability to carry out his job properly, and Madams Mona and Raghda for their failure to adequately police the reading room. Thus, Madam Amal absolved herself from any responsibility for the temporary breakdown of the archive's order, ensuring the security not of the archive but of her own authority and, furthermore, diminishing the standing of her nemesis and underlings.

The director summoned 'Abd al-Rahman to the reading room and gave him and the reading room's assistants a stern lecture about their responsibility for overseeing the security of the archive. Side by side with Madam Amal and in front of all of us researchers, he berated them for their derelictions and declared that such behavior was unacceptable. With her skillful maneuvering, Madam Amal had slipped out of a potentially troublesome situation with her power not only intact but elevated, as she stood literally on the side of the director against her assistants and 'Abd al-Rahman. For their part, they accepted the blame because they knew that someone had to take it, that there would be no real consequences after this scolding, and that this public shaming was a necessary performance to restore the institution's order after a disturbance.

For us researchers, the whole affair resulted in the return of the archive's stricter security regime. Once again, no pens or bound materials were allowed in the reading room. Personal belongings were checked numerous times. Pages were counted. More onerous than all these measures—which, in truth, served useful purposes—was the shadow of distrust, suspicion, and anger that fell over the reading room. Madam Amal leaned on researchers ever harder. Because, as in the rest of Egypt, so much of the function of this government institution rested unquestionably in the person of a single individual, even one unprivileged outside her realm, her capricious moods and opinions determined most everything that occurred in the reading room. Even more than before, she was short with everyone, yelled at us for trivial things, and hovered over us as if we were inmates in a prison. Collective policing and punishment was the logical outcome of a generalized security regime. If every citizen represented a potential threat to order and stability, then all had to be surveilled, disciplined, preempted, and, if need be, eliminated.

Just as the populace at large resented the government's draconian management of their lives, so too my fellow researchers and I chafed at the archive's post-theft regimen of mass punishment. All researchers understood the imperative for reasonable security protocols, but the criminalization of the historians had gone too far. After about two weeks of this harsher regime, my frustration and resentment at being treated as a potential—or, indeed, it seemed at times already convicted— thief boiled over. It was far from my finest moment, but it is instructive. One day at about five in the afternoon, after seven hours of work, I was tired and ready to leave. Once my loose sheets of paper and pencil were inspected in the reading room, I walked out to the small storage room to get my bag. I found the room locked, a not uncommon occurrence as the attendant often left to go to the bathroom, pray, or hang out with friends elsewhere in the building. Only she possessed the key, which she kept on her person at all times, retrieving it each morning from the security office in the basement and leaving it there at the end of the day. No one could access the room in her absence; one had to wait for her return, and so I did. The last thing a researcher who has spent an excruciatingly long day sitting in the reading room wants is to spend another second in the archive's un-air-conditioned second-floor lobby. After about twenty minutes, I began inquiring as to where the attendant might be. I asked at the café, went back into the reading room to see if the afternoon staff knew anything, and called down to the main security desk—all to no avail. Another forty minutes later, she appeared.

I was livid. How could she have just abandoned her post like that? And for so long! She ignored me as she opened the door. Her silence angered me more; I grabbed my things and turned to leave. I had allowed the afternoon shift worker in the reading room to look through my papers all he wanted, but having waited an hour already, I was in no mood to remain in the storage room while the attendant looked through my papers again. However, to follow the rules and hoping to avoid an argument, I held my stack of papers in front of her and fanned through them so she could see that I had taken nothing from the reading room. Invoking the authority of her position and no doubt because I had yelled, she demanded to hold the papers herself to inspect them. "Why?" I exhaled in frustration. I had just shown her that I did not have any archival materials hidden among my papers. She insisted. I refused. We now crossed from the realm of security and procedure into that of ego, respect, rank, and prestige. She felt slighted that I had raised my voice with her. I was angry about having to wait and fed up with the humiliation of being treated like a thief, even after I had shown reasonable proof that I was not. We began shouting back and forth.

I then made my decisive move. Ignoring her demand to inspect my papers further, I collected my things and stormed out of the little storage room. Locking the door behind her, she chased me down the stairs, screaming at me to stop. When I reached the security desk, she was right behind me. The two men at the desk, seeing this commotion coming their way, stood up. I explained myself; she explained herself. They told us to calm down. There was no reason to shout; they did not want any problems. I showed the men my things as required, fanning my papers once more as I had done upstairs in the storage room, desperate to leave the building. Both men seemed satisfied that I had not stolen anything. It helped, no doubt, that they knew and trusted me—even if, again, their security protocols directed them to trust no one. I put my papers in my bag and thought I would finally be able to go home. I snapped rudely at the men, demanding my ID. They told me, again, to calm down, saying that everything had been a bit tense since the attempted theft and that there was no need to get testy. I apologized perfunctorily. I knew I was in the wrong, but the only thing I could think about was leaving. While this exchange was going on, the storage room attendant had taken my ID from the broken desk drawer and was clutching it tightly, clearly not going to give it up. The men told her to let the issue go and to hand me the card. It was over, they said. I had obviously not stolen anything. She refused. She put my ID in her pocket and turned to go back upstairs. This set me ablaze.

I dogged her up the stairs as she screamed back at me that she was reporting me to the director for attempting to bypass security procedures. At this point, halfway up the stairs, shrieking at each other, we made quite a scene and had attracted a small crowd on both the first and second floors. When we arrived at the director's office, we found it locked; he and his staff had already left for the day. The tide turned. As the attendant retreated from the locked door, I followed her, demanding that she give me back my ID. No one was allowed to remove identification documents from the security desk, and indeed it was technically a crime to steal someone's ID card. "Who's the thief now," I barked at her gleefully, hounding her as we went back down the stairs, threatening that *I* would report *her* to the director for leaving her post in the storage room and for stealing my ID from the security desk. I could tell this worried her. When we arrived back at the security desk, she grudgingly pulled my card out of her pocket to give it back to the men stationed there. Before they could react, I snatched it from her hand like a seagull grabbing a sandwich on the beach and stormed out of the building. As she moved to follow me, the men at the desk told her to let me go. It was over. A full hour and a half after leaving the reading room, I was finally out of the building. Neither of us reported the other.

How had I, the patient, discerning historian, become a belligerent, raging man storming out of the building I revered? In my mind's eye, I imagined myself quiet, deliberate, hard-working, an unassuming, reflective, monkish intellectual, ensconced in and consumed by the details of texts. On this day, I was anything but. I had fought and shouted, berated a lowly government employee, and cried out, mostly irrationally, against what I took, rationally, to be an unjust and illogical institution. I was supposed to cradle and love this institution. It was going to make me what I most wanted to be: a historian. Had the archive—that magical land of history- and historian-making, embodied on that day by a humble bureaucrat—failed me? Or, even worse, had I failed it? Failed the archive, failed in being the humble, hushed, meticulous historian, failed personally? My romantic ideal of what it meant to be a historian had crashed into the wall of the actual practice of doing history.

This was a very Egyptian experience. Egypt regularly pushed people over the edge. Beyond the frustrations of unfair rules, terrible working conditions, inefficiencies, and unpleasant interactions, institutions theoretically meant to serve very often came to oppress, squeezing the interest and passion out of people. The Egyptian National Archives naturally attracted those who cared about Egyptian history, sought to devote themselves to it, and showed the drive and ability to contribute to it. Very often, though, this institution that initially drew one in soon repelled and even broke a person, so that he or she wanted never to return. Corollaries of this phenomenon played out across Egyptian governmental, educational, and private institutions. Against the idea of Egypt, the reality of Egypt told a different truth. Inculcated from birth with a love of Egypt, many

Egyptians felt passionate about their country. As they strove to contribute to it, to work, to raise a family, to grow a business, the obstacles of regulation, corruption, lack of opportunity, and inequity inevitably disillusioned many. Even as Egypt expressed pride in itself, it disrespected its people. It endlessly celebrated the nation, even as it imprisoned and tortured its citizens. Egypt drove away some of its best and brightest. Those with means often left the country for good. Those without means grew despondent and retreated into resentment or even depression. For many, the worst part about being Egyptian was Egypt. This more than anything else explains the initial hopes and eventual disappointments of the 2011 uprising.

The rampant and rapacious corruption of Egypt's elite contributed to this despondency, exasperation, and anger. Unlike those of underprivileged university students, some thefts were organized, encouraged, and sanctioned by the state elite. Hierarchy, status, and class determined—as they did in every facet of Egyptian life—who could steal with impunity and who could not. Indeed, part of the definition of power in Egypt was the confidence to steal without compunction. Only the weak were punished, and hence only they worried about consequences.

The former head of the Egyptian National Library perpetrated perhaps the most famous and grievous modern theft of Egypt's unpublished past. In the early 1990s, the library's collection of rare manuscripts—many of them unique copies—moved from its old home in an area near downtown Cairo to share the same building as the archive. The physical transfer of thousands of fragile and precious manuscripts and books was, obviously, an enormous and intricate undertaking. Simply trying to keep track of everything was a herculean task and offered a prime opportunity for theft—and the head of the library took advantage. It is estimated that he arranged for the sale of more than twenty thousand—*twenty thousand*—manuscripts to various libraries and universities in Saudi Arabia. This was theft on an industrial scale, an international project of complex logistical, financial, and bureaucratic organization that surely involved dozens of people in the library administration, officials in the Ministry of Culture, transportation professionals, customs officers, and countless others, all of whom at some point could have tried to stop this stupendous transfer of cultural capital out of Egypt. The man charged with the maintenance, organization, and protection of one of the world's most important collections of knowledge sold it off.

Although Saudi Arabia has long proclaimed itself the cultural and political vanguard of the Arab world, it does not possess the long-standing urban centers and venerable institutions of Egypt or Syria. Over the past decades, it has used its seemingly endless wealth to overcome this deficiency by buying up the heritage and patrimony of the Arab world. An Egyptian bureaucrat sitting on a cultural treasure trove represented an easy target for Saudi bribery. Of course, no punishment for this gargantuan abuse of power ever materialized. Quite the opposite, in fact: the library director spent the rest of his days enjoying a very comfortable life in the Saudi kingdom. The manuscripts stayed there, too.

Contrast this with the experiences of others who stole from the archive or the library. A worker apprehended trying to smuggle out a few documents—underneath clothing or inside pockets—would suffer a temporary cut in his or her already measly pay. (This was for a handful of documents, not twenty thousand complete manuscripts.) Any reduction in pay for governmental employees proved massively consequential for the workers and their families. Yet, as the nearly monthly discovery of registers with ripped-out pages in bathroom stalls—again, some of the few truly private spaces in the archive—attested, many were willing to take their chances of being caught for the potentially high sums these items regularly fetched in Cairo's book markets (still far below those of the overheated illegal Egyptian antiquities trade, but the logic was the same).

The president of the republic and other high government officials—including the director of the national library—regularly stole from the country, every day, in systematic, massive, and truly consequential ways. Their thefts affected Egypt's gross domestic product and the lives of millions of people. And yet, the criminality of the system meant that only those who stole bread to assuage the hunger caused by the corruption of the elite were punished. The stray register in a bathroom stall was the archival equivalent of a loaf of bread. Moreover, if anyone had raised the notion that someone like the director of the national library or any other government official acted corruptly, *that person* would have been considered to be in the wrong, insolent and insubordinate. How could you say that about the director, accuse him of such things? A bureaucrat who stuck his or her neck out to defend an institution from a dishonest director would thus be vulnerable, at fault, and subject to punishment.

The archive seldom fired an employee, though. Researchers were permanently barred. Researchers were annoying and irrelevant, indeed antithetical to the primary purpose of the archive—the jockeying of bureaucrats against one another, the perpetual motion of an ontology of administration. Thefts leading to the removal of researchers therefore proved incredibly productive. Fewer pesky historians meant a lighter workload. The occasional spectacular theft and the dramatic performance of punishment and surveillance that always followed served another vital function, proving what Madam Amal had always maintained—that researchers are suspect and must be guarded against—and hence justifying her authoritarianism.

The only thing standing between the documentation of Egypt's past and an army of outlaws was Madam Amal. She styled herself the archive's defender. Without her, Egypt might lose its history.

Part representing whole, the archive represented Egypt. Madam Amal's defensive posture reflected a wider societal ethos: that Egypt faced ubiquitous dangers and constant assaults from enemies all around. Preemption with arbitrary, gratuitous, draconian, and often ineffective procedures was a necessity. Since the assassination of President Anwar Sadat in 1981, Egypt has been under emergency rule. This forty-year "emergency"—the entirety of the presidency of Hosni Mubarak—justified all sorts of measures to police, oppress, terrorize, and steal from Egyptians. In the 2000s, Egypt cited Islamists and Israel as excuses to do what it wanted; Madam Amal cited those few researchers who stole from the archive. All were (or at least were at one time) real threats, but nowhere near to the extent claimed.

It is important to understand this defensive imperative because it shapes how many Egyptian historians approach archival materials and historical questions. Rarely do historians in Egypt work on a topic that has already been written about. A notion holds that once a subject has been "taken," it is off-limits. The "best" history addresses topics that have never been written about before, using sources that have never been consulted. Conceptual or interpretive innovations are valued, if at all, below a historian's source base. Documents are not completely history, but almost; as such, many believe that once a set of documents has been read, there is no need for anyone else to read them again. Like flour to a baker, they have been used and are gone. The idea that two historians might read the same sources and write two completely different and equally valid histories is a distant one in Egyptian historiography. This attitude leads to the perception of scholarly threats that demands the Egyptian historian's defensive stance. Why would another historian want to consult the same sources or work on the same topic? These are "my" sources. I remember that once a very prominent historian asked to read the still unpublished dissertation of a student who had just completed his degree; in many places such a request would be considered an honor. This student refused out of fear that the professor might cite or discuss documents he had used in his dissertation, rendering his work useless even before it was published. The student thus maintained his own personal security regime around his dissertation, an individual version of the wider social mentality. Much like Egyptian society, Egyptian history consists of many ramparts and moats, with only a few gates and bridges, suspicion prevailing over invitation.

7
Copy Right

The ravenous historian enters the archive seeking nourishment. Despite his weapons of language, paleography, and a deep grounding in historiography, he knows that nothing can fully equip him for the tenebrous dangers that await. The misstep of a misreading can lead him down a murky path of no return; the temptation of what initially appears a lusciously juicy source base may prove poison; the darting slash of a single vicious document can, in an instant, ravage the whole of a historian's corpus. Is there logic to be had in the infinite mess of documents? Only a belief in the possibility of discovery and his ability to impose order on the tangle pushes the historian forward through the thick snarl of forest and underbrush. Collecting archival scraps, the historian amasses a basket of fresh morsels he hopes will sustain him until he lands that perfect kill. Instead of machete and boots, he hunts with paper and pencil (pens are forbidden). His only friends in the foreboding woods are the instruments of his enterprise. What romantic violence it all is.

Unlike some archives, the Egyptian National Archives bars the use of scanners and digital cameras in the reading room, a subset of the general prohibition against photographing what is deemed "sensitive" in Egypt. The researcher's only option is to transcribe materials, relying on pencil and paper or a computer. While the rules against cameras and scanners may at first seem frustratingly cumbersome and archaically slow, they productively compel one to make intellectual choices about what to copy, to ensure that time and effort are spent on a document that will prove absolutely necessary to one's research. One learns to read for utility and quality over possibility and quantity. One is constantly evaluating a source based on the embryonic historical narratives building up in one's head. Recopying a source by hand forces one to understand it completely in the moment, not simply to get an idea about it for potential later use. Transcription is thinking and, ultimately, proves much more productive than the camera's mass capture. Such advantages, though, accrue only after an initial period of struggle and only if one has the luxury of an expansive amount of time to conduct steady work. Without months, really years, in Cairo, archival research proves nearly impossible. In an institution like the National Archives of the United Kingdom, by contrast, one may take countless photographs with a personal digital camera. When I worked there for a week one spring, I left, quite proudly, with ten thousand photos. I only cursorily read a few of these documents at the time to make sure I wanted them and have since read a scant few more. Slow thinking, understanding, and transcribing make for better historians than quick scanning, rapid checking, and partial reading.

One other alternative does theoretically exist in Egypt—photocopying. The photocopier, located in a separate area from the reading room, is the Egyptian National Archives' answer to the digital camera. "Why do you need a camera," Madam

Amal retorted, "when you could photocopy documents?" The photocopier accomplishes several goals for the archive. It allows the institution strict control over its materials and deadens the pace of research. The core logic of any archive is that it possesses documents that *only* exist there, so from the Egyptian National Archives' point of view—always grounded in security—allowing its materials to proliferate around the world through digital reproduction represents an existential threat, akin to theft. If photography were allowed, it would be impossible to control the numbers and uses of those images. The paradigmatic example of the threat posed was always the same: suppose a rich Saudi—the wound of the theft from the national library remained fresh all these years later—financed a few individuals to come to the archive posing as researchers to capture the entire collection. These digital images could then be housed in Saudi Arabia or anywhere else in the world or, worse yet, posted online; they could even be doctored. With Egypt's documentary past freely available to all inside and outside Egypt, what then would be the purpose of the Egyptian National Archives? Of Madam Amal? Of the thousands of others who work in the bureaucracy?

Not just government employees, but most researchers too supported the ban on cameras. Deciphering and understanding complex archival documents is a highly specialized skill won only through discipline and deep study. The camera's quick seizure of yet-to-be-read sources is anathema to the researcher's massive investment of resources. It insults and, more significantly, erodes the researcher's patiently developed comparative advantage. One must sit in the uncomfortable chairs of the archive for years, struggling to read, understand, and transcribe. No other way was thinkable. There was a class argument here, too. Only certain researchers could afford a camera, and therefore allowing cameras would create a gap between those with capital and those without, with this potential inequality greatest between Egyptians and foreigners, who were always assumed to have means, their very presence in Egypt proof of this.

Cameras would also create more work for the primary constituents of the archive: its bureaucrats. As it is now, research grinds along at a laggard pace as researchers read and copy, usually spending one or two days on a single register or box. The fastest might be able to work through two or three registers a day. Were cameras allowed, researchers would turn over materials much more quickly, requesting items more frequently, and would thereby create a higher volume of work for the institution's employees. Faster research in more materials would pressure the staff for increased labor, efficiency, and organization. It might even mean making more of the collection accessible, as researchers would constantly be seeking new materials. No bureaucrat wanted any of this.

When I began my research, the knowledge that my only two options for capturing archival material were transcription and photocopying made me extremely anxious. I knew full well that the former would dominate the latter. To calibrate my expectations, I asked about the options for photocopying. The *lifetime* limit was one hundred photocopies. If I wanted more, I would have to write a formal request to the director of the archive. Resigned to my fate of paper and pencil—typing seemed even slower—I began strategizing how best to organize my work. Should I try to pick representative examples from different periods? Perhaps read a register from every fifth year, or something like that? Or would it be better to find a rich vein and mine that completely? But how would I know what I was missing? The imperative to transcribe thus exacerbated the historian's classic conundrum: breadth or depth? I worked slowly at first, acclimating to the hand, style, and language of my documents. With time, I picked up pace. Court records, for example, all had a standard structure, with distinct and predictable sections. I thus learned to home in immediately on the information I wanted—killing for the choicest meat, ignoring the rest. I began moving at a good clip.

Inevitably, though, I wanted to photocopy certain documents. Some seemed just too long and complicated to copy by hand, others too important to trust to my transcribing. Once dangled in front of me, the possibility of photocopying, however limited and arduous to accomplish, was simply too much to resist. My first itch to photocopy became a rash of trepidation. I knew I had to engage Madam Amal with care and tactful strategy. She could refuse me outright; she did this sort of thing all the time. What would I do then? No recourse seemed possible, so I guessed I would calmly accept. But perhaps I needed to protest, needed to stand up to her early in my time in the archive to gain her respect and, I hoped, eventual help. Was this foolish? Would it backfire on me and forever ruin my relationship with her and thus my chances to photocopy or to do much of anything in the archive? I resolved at least to try. I arose from my chair with a creak to begin my trek to the front of the room, stumbling through the treacherous tangle of my own thoughts.

Whether I liked it or not, my academic future as an Egyptian American student conducting research in Egypt toward an American Ph.D. lay in the hands of an Egyptian bureaucrat. I had invested a lot to be there—fellowship applications, language training, uprooting my life. I missed California and my ex-girlfriend. Why had we broken up? For research, Egypt, Madam Amal? So I could become a historian? How stupid I was. Maybe I could call her. My feet growing colder, I thought to abort my photocopying mission by pretending I was walking toward the door. I arrived at Madam Amal's desk,

smiled, asked how she was. "Fine. What do you want?" As politely as I knew how, I asked if I could please make photocopies
of two pages. She reminded me that for all of eternity I was
allowed one hundred photocopies. I told her that I understood,
that the pages I was requesting were vital to my work, and that
I was ready to count them against my allotted hundred. She
seemed in a good mood that day and told me what to do.

I was to write a formal letter to the director of the archive, making an official request for photocopies of specified
pages in a specified register. She dictated to me the form the
letter should take, and I again transcribed. I was then to place
the letter between the pages of the register. When Madam Amal
was ready and either Muhammad or Radwa was available, the
register and letter would be carried from the reading room to
the photocopy department. Unsure what would happen next
but encouraged that I had come this far, I left the register on
Madam Amal's desk and returned to my seat to wait. After
about thirty minutes, I saw Radwa take the register out of the
room. Another twenty minutes later, Radwa returned with
what I surmised were my photocopied sheets (and my letter)
protruding from the register. The sight of this seemed miracu-
lous, as if the lame had walked again; I prevented myself from
believing it. Madam Amal shook me out of my stunned stu-
por. She directed me to take the request I had written, freshly
annotated by someone in the photocopy department, down to
the bottom floor of the archive, where I would pay for the photocopies. When I returned to the reading room with proof of
payment, I could take the photocopies and the register back to
my desk.

Like much about the archive—and Egypt—the photocopying system was largely opaque. No one ever explained
anything, and one only learned about it through experience,
observation, and eavesdropping on stray conversations. My first

photocopying revealed a few things. I realized, for one, that the letter to the director of the archive was never read by the director; rather, it took the place of a request form. Its primary purpose was to list the requested pages and to provide the staff with a piece of paper on which to write the price of the photo-copying. More than anything else, the letter was the draft of a receipt. An institution whose entire raison d'être is to house paper always seemed to have a shortage of it, and so it fell to the researcher requesting photocopies to provide the paper to fulfill this bureaucratic process.

Moreover, because we were all pretending that the letter was an official request to the director, I had to write it with a pen. Researchers, in theory, were prohibited from writing in ink, but the archive's staff regularly used pens. I asked Madam Amal if I could borrow her pen to write my request, but she told me that at the moment there were no pens in the archive. In the entire edifice, I wondered? Where had they all gone? "What about that one?" I asked. Drained of ink. In the reading room, at least, not a pen was to be found. Madam Amal reas-sured me that more pens were on the way. She added that she and some of the other heads of department had written an of-ficial request (with the pens' last drops of ink?) to the director asking for more. It would be just a few more days. Until then, I queried, was it possible for someone to go to an office supply store and buy a few boxes of pens? This was impossible, I was told, since the staff could only use an authorized brand of pens, and these had to be acquired through official channels. So we waited. During this painful penless period—weeks, not days— the staff constantly asked to borrow the researchers' pens— writing implements that they were forbidden to bring into the reading room. An archive with no pens and no paper—such is the farce produced by Egyptian bureaucracy. As always, peo-ple made do and life went on.

Pages in a register are often unnumbered. How, then, should the researcher list the desired photocopies? Some researchers place torn strips of paper to act as bookmarks for the pages they want. This, though, creates its own kind of confusion. Does the researcher want both pages of the marked spread or just one of them? If there are two bookmarks in a register, does the researcher want all the pages between the two paper strips? Without pagination, the only definite way to ensure that the correct pages are photocopied is for the researcher to go personally to the photocopy room. Given the sensitivities of all that the photocopy room represented, it proved no small matter for a researcher to be allowed into that inner sanctum of toner. Only the most trustworthy and responsible could be considered. Faced with the problem of unnumbered pages on another occasion, I composed my letter to the director and then explained the situation to Madam Amal. I left the register on her desk and returned to my seat, eager for some indication of what would happen next. A couple of hours later, Madam Amal handed the register to Radwa and waved me forward to accompany her to the photocopy department. With my head bowed in deference, I thanked Madam Amal obsequiously and walked several steps behind Radwa out of the reading room. We looked like a funeral cortege, with Radwa carrying the corpse on her outstretched arms to its final home.

Crossing the threshold of the sepulcher of the windowless photocopying room, Radwa placed the register on the desk of one of the department's employees. As I would the few other times I entered this space, I saw the same group of three or four young men in white lab coats, each at his own desk. In another small, dark room beyond them sat the archive's three photocopying machines. One worked better than the others. Here, with the photocopy department functionary, is where I learned most about how the system worked and how best to get what I wanted. The man rarely asked questions, and he was more than happy to break the monotony of the day with some work. If one carefully employed strategic distraction—banter being the most effective—one could even ask for more photocopies than were on the initial request or were officially allowed. One could also tack back and forth, asking for photocopies from the front of the register and then the back, so that there did not seem to be too much photocopying from any one part. The trick, of course, was to get as much as one could without seeming suspicious or greedy.

After completing the photocopying, the man carried the stack of paper back into the front room and handed it to the head of the photocopy department, a woman, who counted the copies and wrote the number on the researcher's request letter, along with the total price. She did not bother to match the number of photocopies actually made with the number specified in the letter. Price was what mattered: copies of different kinds and sizes of documents cost different amounts. (At nearly seventy cents per page, court records were the most expensive.) Leaving the photocopies and the originals with the staff, I took the annotated letter down two stories to the main cashier, who sat in an air-conditioned room with fluorescent lights behind a glass partition of the sort one would find in a bank or a train station. I slipped the paper through a slot at the bottom of the window and the cashier filled out a form in carbon-copy triplicate with my name, the number of copies made, the amount owed, and other information. When I handed over the money, the cashier put it in the top drawer of a broken metal desk that did not lock or even properly close. And, as always seemed to be the case in Egypt, the cashier was eternally short of change. She would often get change from her purse or borrow it from someone else working in the cashier department. Once the fee was paid, she stapled the pink copy of the receipt to the request letter and slipped the yellow copy, un-stapled, between the letter and the pink copy. The white copy stayed with her. I then returned to the photocopy department, where the head bureaucrat kept the original request with the pink receipt stapled to it and gave me the yellow copy as proof of payment. The register stayed in the photocopy room until Madam Amal sent someone to retrieve it.

The pink receipt was the key that allowed the photocopy department bureaucrat—if she ever wanted or needed to—to track a researcher's photocopy total. She threw all of them in a drawer in her desk. To count the total number of copies a researcher made, then, she would have to consult all of a re-searcher's stapled requests and receipts, a procedure that would require some sort of filing system. The cashier with her white receipts could also theoretically do this, but her primary con-cern was the proper collection and processing of payments, not policing the researchers' photocopying tallies. Madam Amal retained no receipts, so despite her repeated dire warnings about a researcher only being allowed one hundred lifetime photocopies, she had no way to track and enforce this herself. Money makes bureaucracy abound in Egypt. From mundane purchases to donations at a saint's tomb, whenever money is involved, one must bounce from place to place, usually with multiple pieces of paper bearing the signatures of various indi-viduals, to complete a transaction.

With its many protocols, forms, steps, and participants, such labyrinthine bureaucratic density creates manifold op-portunities for bribery, privilege, deception, the blustering of authority, favoritism, subterfuge, and the arbitrary application of rules. One of the many ways this manifested in the archive was the entitlement certain researchers received to photocopy at will, with no written request—indeed, without even getting up from their chairs. When one of Egypt's most eminent historians wanted photocopies, his proved a radically different procedure from everyone else's. Instead of writing a formal request, he simply listed the pages he wanted from *multiple* registers, and then Muhammad or Radwa took the materials and list of page numbers to the photocopy room. Leaving aside any other work they might have had, they devoted themselves to this one historian's photocopying and, with model efficiency, returned promptly with a thick stack of photocopies and told the historian how much he owed—generally not an insignificant sum, given the scale of the copying. The historian handed over the money and then the employee, not the historian, went downstairs to pay, returning with change and a receipt and receiving a nice tip. All of this unfolded in front of the rest of us plebeian researchers, and of course Madam Amal, with nary a whiff of anything awry. The historian kept working and left the reading room with hundreds of photocopies.

Such injustice occurred all over Egypt every day; the surfeit of supposedly concrete rules that crushed most enabled the privileges of a few. In the archive, this classed politics of photocopying directly shaped the writing of Egyptian history, the nature of historiographical debate, and the possibilities for our collective understanding of the past. Capturing in ink more photocopies than anyone else—by having the financial means and the dispensation to do so and therefore, we must say, doing less mundane labor than anyone else—the advantaged historian could write different histories than the rest of us. He had more documents at his disposal, and so, from the comfort of his home study, he could refer back at any moment to an exact copy. He never had to choose which documents to copy (forget the drudgery of transcribing) and which to skip. His technique was closer to the British model—copy everything and *then* go through it at leisure. While I do not know this for sure, he conceivably could have possessed copies of entire registers; he regularly took home two hundred photocopies on a single day. The previously stated concern that camera usage would offer unfair research advantages to the rich over the poor had evidently evaporated. Was not paying for limitless photocopies the same thing? Of course, those with social status, money, and authority tend to support the system that affords them these benefits. The Egyptian historical establishment rewards historians who offer triumphant narratives about the Egyptian nation with easier and greater access to archival documents so that they can continue that story. Why give documents to those of oppositional political persuasions or to individuals from the wrong university, a former or current colonial power, or the lower classes?

Destruction is inherent in the practice of history. As animals kill to eat, historians consume archives to sustain themselves. Over the course of each day in the archive, small piles of broken-off bits of archival materials collect on the desk of each researcher. The janitors usually sweep these shards of centuries ago to the floor and then vacuum them up. Registers and boxes move from room to room on rickety old metal carts, carried by hand, or sometimes balanced on people's heads. They are thrown and stacked, smashed and forced open. Only the most violent treatment attracted admonishment from a bureaucrat or a researcher. Never mind the musty, moist basement storage rooms in which the materials live—as the use of materials does, their "preservation" also slowly destroys them. Given these realities, what is the historian's responsibility? If the reading of archival materials damages them to the point of eventual destruction, should they be read? Which is more important—that a historian capture the content of a document or that it remain intact for the future? What good is an archival document if it is never read (if a source falls in the forest . . .)?

What does it mean for history if, after a source is used and cited, it can never be consulted again? What is the ethical practice? Leaving aside questions about the potential of digital technology for preservation, what are we as historians to do with the fact that our very practice leads to the physical sacrifice of the documents on which we all rely?

On one of the few other occasions I was able to photocopy, I faced an egregious instance of this conundrum of archival destruction. I again followed Radwa out of the reading room as she carried my unpaginated register to the photocopy department. When we arrived in that temple of replication, she handed it over to one of the men in lab coats. I had worked with him before. He took the register to the back room with me eagerly in tow. I showed him the pages I wanted as we talked about the Egyptian national soccer team's recent loss to Algeria. He worked as we spoke; I watched closely to make sure he captured all the text I needed. Pleased with his copy of the first page, I showed him the next portion I wanted: a two-page spread. He adjusted the machine's settings for this wider original. And then he did something that made my stomach jump into my throat. Holding the open register face up like a baby at its baptism, in one swift motion he cracked its spine, and, before the croak could leave my mouth, he had flipped the register over and slammed it down onto the glass of the photocopy machine. In a mushroom cloud of archival debris, I saw the clean break down the full length of the binding. I lunged at the register in helpless disbelief, obviously too late.

"What are you doing?" I screamed.

He looked at me with innocent eyes and asked back, "What? Didn't you want the entire spread?"

"Yes, but not like this, not at the expense of the register. That is more than two hundred years old!"

"Well, I just wanted to make sure I got all the text," he said, passing the fault to me for asking for the photocopy and then overreacting.

He did indeed succeed in capturing all of the text. At what cost? The carcass of the register now lay in two nearly separated halves. What had I done, I thought to myself. Would I be the last person on earth ever to read this source? Did it now exist only on the photocopied sheets I would take home with me and then bring to the United States? The weight of all of this hit me hard—the decimation, seizure, removal, guilt, responsibility. By contrast, those around me in the photocopy room seemed unbothered. Was a cleaved register a regular happening for them? If the photocopy technicians, the archive's reproductionists in lab coats, repeated what had been done to my register even just a few times a week, it would not be long before much of the collection was in tatters. I the historian had been an unwilling accomplice to this wrongdoing, at the very least an enabler of obliteration. Surreal and criminal deed done, part of me felt obligated to try to impress upon the man that he should be more careful with such fragile objects. Another part of me, though, felt deep ambivalence about doing this. I did not want to partake of the colonial attitude that told Egyptians to care more about their heritage. In the nineteenth century, Europeans justified their pillaging of pharaonic antiquities by claiming that they appreciated them more than Egyptians did. "Look how they let them languish. We can preserve them for all of humanity." Was the archive for Egyptians (and which Egyptians?) to do with as they wanted—preserve, destroy, or anything else they chose? Or did this past belong to others as much as it did to Egypt? Was preservation a universal ideal or locally defined, and who decided?

For myself, I vowed that I would never photocopy again. I could not control what others did, but I would do my best not to participate in the ruination of archival documents. But what about my research? Others enjoyed the advantage of photocopying, even in wild contradiction of the rules. If the archive allowed me to photocopy, why should I give up even my paltry one hundred pages? Perhaps this was simply how *real* historians did things? Would I be stupid *not* to photocopy? What was the ethical stance? Sacrifice the archive for my own selfish professional and intellectual pursuits, or sacrifice whatever profit photocopying afforded me to protect the archive? It seemed to me that most historians chose the former. Rather than precluding their entry into the guild, their devouring of archival documents seemed, in fact, to open doors for them. I should do that too then, right? Even if the destruction of the register upset me, I was competitive, young, ambitious. I had to have archival materials for my work. So I would not stop requesting photocopies, then?

Archival documents are the historian's sustenance. We hunt.

8
Errata

During the course of my research, Egypt changed the weekend. Historically Thursday and Friday, it became Friday and Saturday. As the day of the weekly Muslim prayer, Friday is clearly a day off, a day like no other. Private companies and government offices close, and schools take off as well. It is difficult to get a refrigerator repaired on a Friday or to go to the doctor. Part of Friday's uniqueness derives from the draining of the city's traffic on that day. In contrast to the intense congestion of the other six days of the week, Cairo on Fridays feels deserted. Traffic— the time it demands, the stress it causes—shapes much of life in Cairo; indeed, it is difficult to exaggerate just how much traffic determines in the city. Four-hour commutes are common. People have learned how to live in traffic—to eat, conduct business, groom, and shop—and to die in it, as ambulances gain no advantage from their sirens. Scheduling anything in Cairo is an exercise in estimation. Friends often agree to meet at two or three, which means they will likely see each other at four.

Fridays represent a release from all of this—from commuting, work, responsibility, the headaches of daily life. People sleep in, go to the mosque, exercise, or stay at home with their families for a nice meal. Many take advantage of Cairo's relative emptiness to ride bikes, picnic, walk, or otherwise enjoy outdoor activities made unpleasant on the other six days by the city's pollution, noise, and traffic.

Which day should complete the weekend proved less clear. For government institutions, it was Thursday, when most either closed altogether or operated on a highly abbreviated schedule. Some schools observed Thursday as a weekend day, and others Saturday. Most multinational corporations took Saturday off to match more closely the weekend in Europe, the United States, and most of Asia. For the same reason, some foreign companies took the unusual step of forcing employees to work on Fridays, offering a weekend of Saturday and Sunday. Apart from these exceptions, Sunday was a workday, although many offices allowed their Christian personnel to take part of Sunday morning off so they could attend church. Thus, depending on one's job and religion, the weekend was some combination of Thursday, Friday, Saturday, and Sunday.

As a government entity, the archive observed a weekend of Thursday and Friday. Thursday operated as a half day with limited services, similar to the afternoon shift after Madam Amal, her staff, and others left—a chance for government employees to work extra hours—and many of the afternoon staff did, in fact, take the Thursday morning shift. Researchers could not request new items on Thursdays, nothing came up from storage, and the café and photocopy room were closed. For university professors and other professionals who worked Saturday through Wednesday, Thursday morning offered them their only chance to visit the archive, so one would see a different group of researchers that day. With the café quiet, fewer people in the building overall, and a self-selected group of focused and diligent researchers, Thursdays were generally a calm and peaceful time in the reading room.

In the spring of 2006, Mubarak's government issued a decree declaring that henceforth the weekend in all government offices would be Friday and Saturday, with Thursday now a full workday. The primary motivation for this was the desire to standardize the work week throughout Egypt, so as to allow companies, schools, government offices, and mosques and churches to coordinate more effectively with one another and align more closely with work schedules outside Egypt. Secondarily, standardizing the work week, it was thought, would relieve some of the traffic pressure in Egypt's major cities. If the bulk of Egyptians took Saturday off, then it would be more like Friday, the hope went, thereby offering people another day of low traffic and potential leisure.

Declaring a uniform weekend, and hence work week, represented a fundamental transformation in people's personal and professional lives, with implications for institutional planning, organizational structures, meeting and pay schedules, media, calendar design, bus and train timetables, vacation plans, and much more. Revamping such a seemingly natural thing as the weekend—a feature of life most of us take as a given—reveals just how arbitrary it and our reliance on it truly are. There is, of course, nothing inherent in either Thursday or Saturday being a weekend day. The case is easier to make for Friday or Sunday (or Saturday in Israel), but, upon reflection, one sees that even this is a construction born of intentional human design. The division between work week and weekend is a product of modern industrial capitalism and its disciplining of time toward the goals of productivity, commerce, and planning. By changing the week's balance of days, the Egyptian state not only exposed the artificiality of time and the contested nature of capitalist organization, but—more to its real objective—proved its infinite power to melt down and remold the seemingly iron-cast with the stroke of a pen.

The archive handled the transition exceedingly well. Bureaucrats and researchers adjusted their schedules, and everything moved smoothly once the new weekend took hold. Saturday now operated as Thursday had—a half day with limited staff and services. A month or so after the change, I planned to come in for my first of the new Saturdays. That week, I had only worked three days and was feeling guilty; a half day on Saturday would help to make up for my lackluster schedule. I resolved to arrive early, around 10 a.m., and to work until I was kicked out, probably at around 3 p.m. Although the archive technically opened at 9:15, workers usually arrived late—traffic— and most researchers did not start trickling in until about 9:45. Thus, 10 a.m. felt late enough to ensure that the reading room would be open and fully functioning but still early enough to allow for a full day of research.

I climbed the archive's steps a little before 10. When I reached Ahmed at his security desk, it became immediately apparent that something was amiss that Saturday. Fifteen or so of my fellow researchers—regulars and those who could only come in on off-days—were milling about, chatting. Ahmed informed me that the bureaucrat who was responsible for the reading room that day had not appeared yet. He was supposed to have arrived between 9 and 9:15, but there was still no sign of him. This, of course, annoyed and frustrated us researchers to no end, as we had organized our day—our lives—around working in the archive during certain hours. We discussed what to do, cursing the bureaucrat and our fate. "We are all waiting for this one person," someone said in exasperation to Ahmed, the only authority figure around. "Why should all of us be made to suffer because he is late?"

This sort of thing occurred every day all over Egypt. Buses, people, letters, money, solutions, and hope proved consistently late. In situations like this, two viable options, with their advantages and disadvantages, presented themselves: forgo or wait, go home or stay. If I leave, I can stop wasting time and instead do something productive, salvaging something of the day. The fear, though, is that as soon as I leave, the government employee will arrive, and I will therefore have squandered the time invested in commuting and waiting: "If only I had waited just a bit longer." But how long is too long? For some, leaving is not an option. If Saturday is one's only possible day to work in the archive, or if one has spent two hours in the commute, leaving empty-handed feels especially cruel. For these researchers, waiting with the faintest possibility of even an hour of work is the only sensible thing to do. The disadvantages of waiting are obvious: time lost, frustration, the risk that the person will not come for hours or may never come.

I had committed to working that Saturday morning and so decided to wait. Helpless and with no idea how long our wait would be, we did what we could to improve the situation. "Can't you call him," we implored Ahmed, "to see where he is?" Ahmed did not know his number. He kept saying, as Egyptians often did in these situations, that the bureaucrat would be here soon, he was on his way, not to worry, only a few more minutes now, no doubt. Ahmed, needless to say, knew no more than any of us. At some point during our purgatory, I asked him if the archive ever punished workers for tardiness or anything else. Sometimes, he said, mostly by docking their pay. He added that he was personally going to report this bureaucrat. Everyone understood Cairo's traffic situation and expected—and could therefore be flexible about—lateness, to a degree. The line between acceptably late and too late was clearly a subjective one, and Ahmed believed the bureaucrat had crossed it. His assertion that he would report his fellow worker was no trifling matter. Within the structures of the Egyptian bureaucracy—a constantly shifting world of jockeying, cooperation, and competition among workers at different levels of authority—such an act was an escalation that could have potentially lasting and deeply negative consequences not only for the individuals involved but for the entire system. All bureaucrats, even those who despised one another, shared a common interest in diminishing expectations. Come late, leave early, work slowly, more breaks, more workers. The understandable goal was to grind work down to its minimum efficiency. Government pay was too abysmal to elicit anything more. Reporting those engaged in these behaviors threatened a response from administrators that could damage the overall objective of decreasing the demands on workers. This was therefore generally to be avoided.

We continued waiting. "Can't someone else monitor the room until he arrives? What's the big deal, really? He doesn't do anything anyway. We just need someone to sit there." The Saturday bureaucrat's main job, as on weekday afternoons, was to sit in the reading room to ensure that no one stole anything or caused a problem. His role required no particular training, technical expertise, or deep well of experience. He signed out the reading room key, went upstairs, unlocked the room, turned on the lights, and then sat in Madam Amal's chair for five hours.

To our question about why another employee could not unlock the reading room and sit there until the late bureaucrat arrived, Ahmed replied that it was impossible (*mayinfahsh*). Bureaucratic logic tasked every government employee with a specific job each day, even if it required no particular skill or ability, or even, in truth, if it was not necessary to the institution's function. Everyone slotted in somewhere. Thus, if someone left his post to sit in the reading room, then he would be

committing the double transgression of shirking his own responsibilities and taking someone else's job. Moreover, when
the original bureaucrat discovered this usurpation, he would
no doubt be furious and accuse the person of trying to steal
his job and his pay (since it was an off-day, pay on Saturdays
was slightly higher than normal), and all of this could get very
messy if it were to bubble up through the administrative ranks.

General unwillingness to bend the bureaucracy of the
archive, despite common sense, derived from bureaucrats' deep
and logical desire to avoid taking responsibility. Responsibility
opened the door to trouble and blame. By design of the bureaucracy, however, the archive deliberately charged each individual worker with the responsibility of an aspect of its function. On this Saturday, the late bureaucrat was freighted with
the reading room. Only he could sign out the key. Only he
could sit at the front of the room. Were anything to go wrong
that day, he would be held responsible and punished. (Suc-
cesses, by contrast, belonged to the institution, never the individual.) By making an individual responsible for everything
within his or her purview at all times, the state bureaucracy
pinned all its problems on the inabilities, incompetence, or
mistakes of a single person, exculpating the system even as the
problem *was* the system.

The clock slowly ticked past 10:30. We had all already
given Ahmed our identification cards. He had recorded our
information and given us the plastic permits that served as our
daily research passes. All we needed was the bureaucrat to let
us in. At a few minutes to 11, he limped up the staircase and
into the building. Ahmed, another bureaucrat who had come
to hang out with him, and some researchers crowded around
the man in anger, frustration, and relief, jostling and harangu-
ing him: "Where have you been? We've all been waiting!"

The man looked flustered. With quickened breath, he told

us that the microbus he'd been riding to work had had an accident and his foot had been injured, hence his tardiness and the limp. Others had been injured too. It was not his fault that he was late, he declared. Keen to absolve himself of blame, he attempted to turn the tables by suggesting that he had sacrificed his body in coming to the archive at all. He should have gone to the hospital to have his foot examined, he told us, but he did not want to miss work. In an awesome show of indifference and insensitivity, no one seemed to believe the man's story or care about his limp, which most of us took to be feigned. Everyone just wanted him to get upstairs as quickly as possible to open the reading room.

We moved in a pack around the hobbling bureaucrat up the stairs to the reading room. He opened the door, and we poured in past him toward the registers and boxes on the front shelves. Despite the seemingly interminable wait, it was only a little past 11, still early enough to get in a few good hours before the 3 p.m. fire alarm signaled the day's end. The bureaucrat staggered to Madam Amal's chair, and, like my fellow researchers, I took my register from the shelf behind him. I plopped down at the first free desk, not far from where the bureaucrat sat, attending to his foot.

I found the place in the court register where I had stopped reading a couple of days before and picked up from there. After about half an hour, I noticed the bureaucrat reciting snatches of the Quran under his breath. With no newspaper to read and no one to talk to on the phone, evidently, he was passing the time. He perched his chin on his crossed hands, leaning on the bare desk. His voice was muffled, but sonorous enough to carry to where I sat. As soon as my ear latched on to his mellifluous recitation, my mind could not let it go. I tried to tune it out, but I found myself following along instead of focusing on the words in front of me. Should I ask him to stop or to mumble more quietly? Would this anger him, cause a fight, and hence be even more disruptive? Given his tardiness and who he was (namely, not Madam Amal) and realizing that now I was thinking more about the noise itself and about whether or not to ask him to quiet down than about the register in front of me, I resolved to ask him politely to please speak more softly. Before I could, though, the man stopped, and so I was, thankfully, saved from myself.

Reading room opened, recitation concluded, research moving along now: despite the morning's stumbles, the day had been salvaged. I found cases relevant to my research and, rigorous historian that I was trying to be, a proper striver in late capitalism, I copied them dutifully. It was now past 1 p.m. As I was in the middle of transcribing a case, suddenly there was darkness; the lights had gone out. The piece of property I was reading about would have to wait to be sold. I dropped my pencil and thought to myself that this day was cursed indeed. Would the lights only be out for a few minutes? For the rest of the day? Should I wait? For how long? Should I just leave now? The waiting game restarted. Many of us gathered at the front of the room to talk, complain, and pool our hopes that the electricity would come back on.

We waited. After about twenty minutes, we concluded that the electricity might be out for some time. Several researchers continued to work in the dark, either using the screens on their phones for light or simply allowing time for their eyes to adjust to the thin daylight seeping in through the windows in the corner of the room. More of a concern was the absence of air conditioning. With midday temperatures in the eighties in late April, the bodies in the reading room soon made the air sticky and warm. As I thought about whether or not to leave, accepting this day as a defeat, I noticed that some researchers had picked up their desks and moved them next to the windows. Given the regime of order that ordinarily ruled the archive, this action shocked me. The desks had seemed to me fixed in the earth, features of an unchangeable geology. It was a brilliant move born of the logic of necessity and assisted by the laxity of Saturday. Egypt's Orwellian bureaucracy often birthed such creativity as people circumvented the state. Perhaps because he understood the sense this made, perhaps because he was embarrassed to have been so late, and probably because he knew he could not stop us, the bureaucrat did nothing to prevent us researchers from undertaking this clearly forbidden act.

I asked a friend to help me move my desk. To maximize the number of us that could benefit, we crowded our desks together near the windows in a kind of wooden Pangaea. Some shared a desk, some even shared a chair. Here we were, about twelve historians (all men) crowded together with our registers and boxes almost touching in the corner of the darkened archive. It felt intimate—medieval, basic, and comforting in our monkish proximity. In the direct and drenching sunlight, close together, with no air conditioning, we all grew hotter than warm. Even so, the situation was a refreshing—if momentary—contrast to the normally antiseptic mood of the archive, with its fluorescent lighting and the archipelago of desks isolating us from one another. We worked united like this for the remaining few hours of the day, joking and laughing about things we found in our documents, making fun of the day's bureaucrat, other employees of the archive, and one another. Even as we talked and riffed, we continued to work: transcribing and teasing, concentrating and chortling.

Although this Saturday was mostly a day of frustration and wasted time, I cherished those few sweaty, convivial hours I spent with my fellow researchers in the corner of the room. We shared a camaraderie that I rarely experienced in the ar-

chive, the sort of amity that comes only from collectively facing and overcoming hardship, however minor. As 3 p.m. approached, the electricity remained off. The fire alarm (powered
by a generator or battery?) rang to signal the end of the day.
We moved the desks back to their original positions, returned
our registers and boxes to the shelves, and filed out. Behind us,
the bureaucrat flipped off the light switch, to ensure the darkened room stayed dark.

9
Images

One of the more disconcerting conversations I had in the archive resulted from a mistake I made in addressing Rasha, the researcher whose spat with Laura and then Madam Amal occasioned the "Rules of the Reading Room." I did not know Rasha well. Our relationship consisted of some polite hellos and goodbyes and sometimes sitting in the same group during breaks. Unthinkingly, perhaps because of her age, I always, with respect, referred to her as *Ustaza* (Professor) or *Doktora* (Doctor) Rasha. One day over tea in the café, she ground the light banter to a halt with the rebuke that she was neither a professor nor a doctor and I must stop calling her that. The group turned first to her, then to me. I apologized for addressing her with these honorifics (it could be worse, I thought) and promised to call her by her name only from then on. The implication of her peeved comment was that I was making fun of her and, though I was doing nothing of the sort, I understood her point. She did not want to be singled out from the other researchers for

being older and richer, or a wife and mother. She was as professionally titleless as the rest of us.

Nearly a year later, Rasha called me out of the blue. Since
the cell phone forms part of one's identity in Egypt, we had
exchanged numbers soon after meeting. Still, I was surprised
when I saw her name flashing on the tiny screen of my Nokia
3310. We had never spoken on the phone before. We exchanged
the customary courtesies and questions: how is your work,
where have you been, we miss you, how is your family, and so
on. She rang me, so she was paying for the call. The breeziness
of our conversation, her obvious lack of urgency, again marked
her as a person with a degree of wealth and status—someone
who did not have to think about her phone bill. After these
pleasantries, she arrived at the purpose of her call. "Do you
want to be on television?" Pause. This was not a question I,
a history graduate student, had ever been asked. My initial
thought was *of course* I want to be on television! Is there anyone who *doesn't* want to be on television? In Egypt as in most
places, television played a central role in people's lives. Perhaps
more particular to Egypt was the outsized function of television in the inculcation of national and regional culture. Historically, the government controlled the ten channels available
in Egypt, directing their content toward political and educational ends. These ten channels remain stalwart today, but satellite television now offers hundreds of stations from around
the world. The government, too, has taken advantage of the
opportunities afforded by satellite to create a slew of new stations and programming.

Playing it cool, I prodded Rasha for details. One of the
new government-run television stations, al-Thaqafa (Culture),
aired an occasional program entitled *Qissat Watha'iq* (A Story
of Documents) that showcased historians presenting archival
documents. Each episode revolved around a single topic, edu-

cating Egyptians about an important aspect of their history and revealing something of how historians worked. The program was planning a show on the history of the Mahmudiyya Canal, which runs from the Nile to Alexandria. As Alexandria, Egypt's second city and most important Mediterranean port, had no natural link to the Nile and hence to much of the rest of Egypt, governments since the Greeks have attempted, with varying degrees of success and mostly failure, to connect the city to the Nile valley via a canal. Rasha knew I was working on issues related to irrigation and had recently given a talk at the French Institute in Cairo on the history of the Mahmudiyya Canal in the early nineteenth century. She told me she had been on *Qissat Watha'iq* before and knew the host and some of the production team—further evidence of her connections; unlike most researchers in the archive, Rasha knew important people. Given Rasha's dissertation research on Alexandria, the host had asked her if she knew anyone who could join her on the show to speak on the history of the canal.

Although I did indeed work on the history of the canal, that was not the primary reason Rasha chose to call me. Because of the prominent status of television in Egypt—even of sparsely watched shows like those about archival documents—Rasha's invitation was a gift of prestige. Such a precious social commodity had to be managed with care, and it was a shrewd calculation to offer the break to me. I was not like other researchers. I had no real connections to the Egyptian university system, did not live in Egypt permanently, and would leave at some point. I was therefore a safe choice. Any status I gained by being on television would pose no potential competitive disadvantage for Rasha in the race for publication or employment opportunities or professional connections. As an Egyptian American, I was an outsider playing a very different professional game.

If anything, the fact that I was a foreigner helped Rasha in the inexorable contest for cachet. Having American or European friends represented social capital, so her ability to produce an American for the show evidenced her stature. Rasha was using me to burnish her reputation as a member of a global network of historians. Moreover, in being introduced on television as an American who had come to Egypt to study its history, I would bolster nationalist claims about the importance of Egypt and its place in the history of the world over millennia: "Look, even an American recognizes Egypt's splendor and majesty." Of course, I did think Egyptian history was significant—I was in the process of dedicating my life to it— but not in the ways nationalist historians and popular culture made it out to be. I did not believe that something innate or eternal in Egypt's character somehow resulted in its central place in world history; rather, I sought explanations in the contingent histories of Egypt's economy, politics, demography, and geography. How does one argue for importance, even uniqueness, without falling into brute nationalism?

I agreed to participate, and Rasha filled me in on the details. The shoot was the next day. So soon! I was to meet her and the production team at 7 a.m. in front of the central television building, which was, conveniently, less than a kilometer from the Egyptian National Archives. We would then travel as a group to film along the canal and end at its terminus in Alexandria. Rasha told me to bring copies of documents about the history of the canal and to prepare what I would say. She would talk about the canal from its earliest beginnings through the late Mamluk period; I was to concentrate on its history during the Ottoman period, my area of expertise.

After getting off the phone, I scrambled to figure out which documents to bring. Given the near unattainability of photocopies in Egypt, I did not know whether I had any rele-

vant sources to show (my handwritten transcriptions would obviously not make for compelling television). Thumbing through
the photocopies in my files, I found two that dealt squarely
with episodes in the canal's reconstruction in the early nineteenth century. There was a snag, though: the documents were
from the Ottoman archives in Istanbul (where photocopies
were more easily obtained), not from the Egyptian National
Archives, and they were written in Ottoman Turkish rather
than Arabic. In Egyptian historiography, the dominant school
of thought viewed the Ottomans as an occupying power—
violent, extractive, paternalistic, and repressive. Much of my
dissertation work attempted to think beyond simple narratives
of Ottoman oppression or benign rule to examine the me-
chanics of imperial governance in Egypt, to show how the
empire shaped Egypt and Egypt the empire, and, moving past
facile value judgments, to soberly analyze the gains and losses
occasioned by Egypt's nineteenth-century separation from the
empire. These two documents spoke to a tiny sliver of this
larger interventionist project.

Specifically, the documents addressed the repairs to the
canal that began in 1817, by order of the Ottoman governor
Muhammad 'Ali. Egyptian nationalist historians and most
Egyptians consider Muhammad 'Ali "the founder of modern
Egypt." A common refrain asserted that Muhammad 'Ali began
the project of modern Egypt and Nasser finished it. (One of
the many realities glossed over by this narrative of the two
behemoth bookends of Egypt's modern history is that Nasser's
Free Officers overthrew Muhammad 'Ali's descendants.) Muhammad 'Ali, the story goes, built roads and schools and challenged the Ottoman Empire, winning freedom and glory for
Egypt. My research contributed to a growing wave of work
that challenged this national myth, showing that Muhammad
'Ali did not seek to "liberate" Egypt toward any sort of nation-

alist end but rather hoped to secure the territory as an independent holding for himself and his family. He did not love
Egypt or Egyptians; in fact, he despised his subjects. He was
born in Kavala (today in Greece) and was posted to Egypt as
an emissary of the Ottomans. He never learned Arabic; he saw
Egypt as merely a stepping stone in his own imperial designs
of grandeur.

Nationalists usually pointed to attempts to restore the
Mahmudiyya Canal as evidence of his efforts to improve the
infrastructure and agricultural potential of Egypt—and the repaired canal did indeed increase the acreage of irrigated land
near its banks and contributed to a population boom in Alexandria. But the canal's overhaul also produced a massive pile
of bodies. Muhammad 'Ali forcibly moved more than 300,000
Egyptian peasants (a number that exceeded Cairo's total population at the time) to work on the canal. More than 100,000
of these workers—the equivalent of 40 percent of Cairo—died
from exhaustion, accident, heat, and disease as they dug, dredged,
reinforced, and cleaned the canal. My research thus challenged,
or at least complicated, the idea that Muhammad 'Ali was some
great founding father of modern Egypt.

Would such a revisionist narrative work for a television
audience accustomed to the nationalist story? I did not know.
But, I thought, if this story was important enough for me to
invest a decade of my life to research and tell it, then I should
be ready to take it to a mass audience. Nonetheless, I understood that my position as a foreign researcher in Egypt, an
American no less, was a double-edged sword. Yes, my Americanness evidenced Egypt's singular glory—so majestic that it
drew scholars from across the world!—but, depending on what
I said about Egypt, I could also be viewed as a foreign agent
attempting to malign or damage the beloved country. Even
though I was an Egyptian citizen, I was also the citizen of an-

other country and culturally ambiguous; consequently, my loyalties were impossible to determine and therefore impossible to trust. In pointing to the darker aspects of the repair of the Mahmudiyya Canal, would I be seen as just one more foreigner casting aspersions on the splendors of the nation?

Using Ottoman documents from Istanbul would, I knew, make me especially vulnerable to this charge. Because the dominant nationalist line posited the Ottomans as a colonial power, their documents could not be trusted. No truthful accounting of Egypt would say something as unsavory as that Muhammad ʿAli killed 100,000 peasants. Yet the archival sources, which offered the closest possible version of events, documented this beyond dispute. On a television show about archives, I planned to play the part of the objective historian and let the documents speak for themselves, but I knew that what they said would likely not be heard. The Ottomans had disparaged and oppressed Egyptians in the past, and their documents would be seen as doing the same to Egyptian history in the present. I risked being counted as a party to the conspiracy, an American posing as an Egyptian collaborating with the Ottomans against Egypt. But if I were to have archival documents about the Mahmudiyya Canal by 7 a.m. the following morning, these were my only options. Besides, was it really so radical to present them? What was the worst that could happen? I also needed to spend some time that afternoon on another aspect of my presentation—what I would wear. What was appropriate archival television clothing? What said smart, accessible, objective, trustworthy historian? A suit, clearly, but it was June and too hot for a suit. I settled on a dark, airy button-down shirt and light-colored pants. I shaved.

The next morning, Rasha arrived at the television building fifteen minutes after the appointed time. Like many with means, she enjoyed the services of a driver. She emerged from

the back seat wearing an outfit of multiple animal prints and
more gold jewelry than usual. We walked together to the side
of the building, where the host and crew were waiting. The
seven of us piled into a van (women—Rasha and the host—in
the front, men in the back) at around 7:30. This was still very
early by Egyptian standards, especially during the summer,
when people stay up late to enjoy the cool evenings and then
sleep in. The cameraman drove, taking full advantage of Cairo's
empty streets to speed out of the city proper. With light traffic
on the highway between Cairo and Alexandria, he tore through
the kilometers, darting between lanes, maneuvering the van like
a sports car. Unperturbed by his dangerous driving, I dozed,
my drooping head waking me up every so often. At one point
I awoke suddenly to our van swerving across a lane of traffic
and the host in the front seat shrieking. Being jolted out of my
slumber by this scene frightened me more than if I had been
awake, I think. The crew sitting in the back with me assured
me that the other driver had been at fault and that the cameraman was an excellent driver.

We stopped on the southern outskirts of Alexandria,
near the city's zoo, on a quiet section of the road that runs
alongside the canal, where rows of old, leafy trees offered
much-appreciated shade. The crew had chosen this relatively
secluded location in part because it was likely that no police
would pass by. The show had apparently disregarded the rule
requiring a permit to film on the canal; as it was infrastructure, the canal was considered a "sensitive" area. Given Egypt's
saturation of security, even a show on government television
needed a permit to film and, interestingly, the show's pro-
ducers had decided to skip this bureaucratic technicality altogether. As the crew set up its equipment and shot a series of
long takes panning along the canal, the host explained the plan
for filming. With a microphone clipped to my collar, I was to

stand next to the canal explaining the contents and importance of each document I had brought. I would have fifteen minutes, or longer if I liked. Rasha would do the same. After we finished speaking, we would hold our documents flat against our torsos so the camera could come in close on the text. Once the show was edited, the host told us, in all likelihood the documents would be on the screen most of the time so that viewers could see them, and our explanations would be in voiceover. There would also be some shots of us walking along the canal, as well as sweeping views of the site. In total, there would be thirty minutes of show and tell.

Rasha went first (perhaps an indication that even though I was to refrain from calling her Ustaza or Doktora, I was still to defer to her). She had brought several published maps and copies of documents about the early history of the canal. She explained why the Greeks wanted to build it and why their attempts failed. She talked about the Mamluk sultan Ashraf Qaitbay who, in the late medieval period, named the waterway the Ashrafiyya after himself following a major repair. Finally, she discussed documents from the Egyptian National Archives about the history of the canal and its relationship to the city of Alexandria. She spoke for much longer than fifteen minutes, after which it was my turn. Before presenting my documents, I spent some time, following Rasha's lead, offering general remarks about the history of the canal during the Ottoman period—how peasants petitioned the state to clean the canal, instances of flooding and drought, and disputes over the sharing of the canal's waters. I then launched into a detailed discussion of the documents I brought to display. I spoke for more than fifteen minutes too but for a shorter time than Rasha had.

As a crew member unclipped the microphone from my collar, Rasha announced that she had other documents she wanted to present. Re-outfitted with the microphone and back in front of the camera, she spent twenty minutes analyzing in excruciating minutiae the individual statutes of a trade treaty ratified in the nineteenth century—the period she had asked me to cover—which had little to do with the history of the canal. This struck me as an obvious attempt to replace the potentially problematic challenges to Egypt's national mythology I had offered with a different story about the nineteenth century. Her alternative history had the added benefit of giving her more airtime than I received. Not above petty competition and topical territoriality, I was annoyed by this, but I stood politely to one side as she expounded on the unrelated commercial history of the Mediterranean.

It was now almost noon, and we had finally finished filming. The crew informed Rasha and me that they were going to take advantage of being in Alexandria to shoot additional footage for another show. Rather than waiting to return to Cairo with them, Rasha and I decided to take the train back. The line between Alexandria and Cairo follows a pleasant two-hour course through the agricultural land of the Nile delta. In the taxi to the station, Rasha told me that she had never ridden in a train before and, in fact, that this was her first time in Alexandria. Many Egyptians who can afford to do so avoid trains, so I was not surprised to learn this. I was shocked, though, to hear that she had never been to Alexandria before. She was in her forties and had spent her entire life in Egypt. Alexandria was Egypt's second city, just two hours from Rasha's home in Cairo, and she had a car and a driver. More to the point, Alexandria was the topic of her dissertation. Was she not curious to see the place to which she was devoting years of her life?

During the summers I had spent in Cairo as a kid, my family would often go to Alexandria. Over my past five years in Cairo, I had visited the city probably a dozen times and spent numerous nights there. I liked it and knew parts of it fairly well.

I pointed Rasha to the appropriate ticket window, and she took the next train back to Cairo. I also bought my ticket, but for a train that departed later that afternoon. I walked Rasha to her platform, said goodbye, and went to have fish at one of my favorite restaurants.

Our episode aired nearly six weeks later. Given the unpopular story I told, my use of Ottoman documents, and Rasha's quick-witted provision of alternative material, I fully expected to be cut from the show. However, I was not; I appeared for about a third of the program. My account of the 300,000 laborers made it in, but the death toll did not. Thus, instead of challenging the dominant narrative of Egyptian history by exposing these murders, I was made complicit in them. Unwittingly enlisted to the side of Muhammad 'Ali, I placed these peasant workers on the banks of the canal but was not permitted to tell the truth about their end. I had been cunningly co-opted into a grand story of Egyptian nation building, sublimated into a standard interpretation that buried the ugly bits in the mud. I would rather have been left entirely on the cutting-room floor. This, I learned by losing, is how a dominant narrative dominates.

10

Tables

J ust outside the doors to the reading room was the café, an
L-shaped bar made out of the same grayish white marble
as the floor of the archive building. The bar held a sink
and a two-burner gas stove; sets of glasses, cups, and saucers; spoons; sugar, tea, coffee, and packets of dried milk; sodas;
and, its centerpiece, a tall, battered cylindrical water boiler of
the kind often found in hotel lobbies or restaurants. Tracing
the shape of the bar was a set of four tables, three on the long
side and one on the short, with brick-colored wrought-iron
frames and cracked glass tops. Between ten and twelve chairs
made of the same wrought iron floated around the four tables.
Their seats of crimson vinyl felt cushionless, with rips confirming there was nothing between this outer layer and the
wood underneath. Over the course of the day, the chairs moved
around the café as use dictated, and often someone took one
or more into the surrounding offices—leading, predictably, to
regular arguments.

In the archive, as in much of Egyptian society, a series of

breaks for coffee, tea, and cigarettes punctuated the day. Most researchers took a coffee or, more usually, tea break in the late morning and then again in the late afternoon. Because of limited time or, more often, limited money, not all researchers could afford such breaks, but sometimes, even if someone was not drinking tea or coffee, he or she joined friends for conversation or a smoke. Indeed, these breaks were for rest and socializing more than caffeine or nicotine; they provided a time for researchers to sit together at the same table rather than alone at their desks. Rarely do people drink their caffeinated beverages alone; rarely do Egyptians do anything alone. That is what Americans do.

During my first five years of work in the archive, a group of siblings—three sisters (Hoda, Samah, and Maha) and a brother (Emad)—ran the café, serving Turkish coffee, Nescafé, tea, *yansoon* (anise tea), sodas, and snacks to researchers and employees alike. Outside of formal exchanges, the café was the only venue where these two groups interacted. Not all the caffeine consumed in the archive came from the café, though. Higher-ups like the director and his staff enjoyed the luxury and convenience of a kettle and cups, coffee and tea, in their own offices. Still, sometimes even these lucky few contracted out to the café for their beverages. It was simply easier to be served, and having coffee and tea delivered to them helped to mark their status as the select who never went to the café themselves but had its staff come to them.

Never one to miss an opportunity to assert her dominance, Madam Amal, too, used the café to her advantage. For the obvious reasons—food remnants might attract insects, drinks could spill—food and drink were prohibited in the reading room. As with most rules, however, Madam Amal and her assistants stood above this one, consuming food and drink as a performance of their authority. Emad delivered tea, coffee, sodas, and snacks directly to their desk. In a highly visible display, he would walk the considerable distance from the door of the reading room to Madam Amal's desk, leading with his metal tray, making obvious to us researchers what we could not have. Like a waiter in a restaurant, he would set the drinks and food on the desk, and Madam Amal would thank him in her carrying voice, sometimes asking for other items or why something she wanted was not available. The most pronounced moment in her ritual consumption of tea, soda, and snacks was the final slurp of her straw as she searched for the last few drops of fruity carbonated sugar at the bottom of her soda bottle. Replete, she would summon Emad to retrieve her detritus.

The origins of the café, and how it came to be staffed by the four siblings, dated to the late 1990s, when a large, professionally run cafeteria in the adjoining Egyptian National Library closed for what one assumes were financial reasons. Hoda, one of the café's sisters, had worked there, and, according to her, shortly after it closed she approached the director of the archive with the idea of opening a small café on his side of the building. He saw utility in this, gave her permission, and they shook hands to seal their agreement. I have no reason to doubt Hoda's account, but it seemed out of the Egyptian norm for someone like the head of the archive to allow a poor family he did not know to set up a financial venture in a government institution he oversaw. Much of Egyptian society functions through nepotism, class antagonism, and preferentialism; very rarely do people make it on their own without connections, and even more rarely do those with authority give the poor and unlucky a chance. Perhaps because the family came to the director not as governmental employees with all their promised protections—a contract, guaranteed salary, and other benefits—he felt more ready to offer them space in the archive: it cost him

little and he knew he could get rid of them at any time. The
shield of wealth offers the most safety and security in Egypt,
and being a government bureaucrat provides some modicum
of protection against economic vagaries and injustices. The fi-
nancially most precarious in Egypt were those like the siblings:
freelancers without family capital working outside of government employment.

Whatever its origins, the café represented the family's
main source of income. The four siblings had another sister
and brother. Their father had been the family's primary bread-
winner until he died some years previously, and their mother
suffered from numerous ailments: diabetes, obesity, bad knees,
general ill health. In her sixties, she could hardly stand because
of her weight and weak legs and thus spent most of her time
sitting on the floor of their small apartment's living room, leaning against the couch. Of the two siblings who did not work in
the café, the brother—the eldest child—was unemployed, and
the sister lived with her husband and two children in southern
Egypt. The family members had invested a great deal of their
own capital in the café. The large water boiler, the essential feature of the entire operation, had been their biggest single ex-
penditure. The second was the small gas stove needed to make
Turkish coffee, the most popular item after tea. Their serving
cups, glasses, and saucers did not match, as they had collected
them cheaply where they could. Everything was constantly, as-
siduously cleaned. The siblings purchased every item they sold
and paid for their daily commute. Against these expenses, the
one to two hundred cups of tea and coffee and the snacks they
served each day allowed them to turn enough of a profit to
provide for the family.

The four siblings had been working in the archive for
three years when I arrived in 2001. Conversations with them
were always pleasant, and they maintained amicable relations

with most employees and researchers. They offered a welcome and friendly break from the rigor and, more often, the boredom of archival research. They knew everyone's name and favorite drink. When the café was especially busy and all the chairs taken, I would lean against the bar, as if at a pub, holding my drink or resting it on the bar. Standing at the marble counter, I could see all that went on behind it—the balletic coordination and machinelike efficiency demanded by the tight quarters—and chat with the siblings as they worked. Conversation never seemed to distract them. Two of the sisters prepared drinks behind the bar, while Emad and the third sister delivered them on metal trays to the tables and to offices throughout the building, returning with new orders.

This comfortable daily rhythm disintegrated in the early summer of 2006. I had come to the archive as usual that morning and noticed that the bar area was empty. I assumed that my friends were running late, as one does in Cairo. When I left the reading room a little before noon for my first break of the day, I thought surely they would have arrived. But the area was still empty. I asked what was going on and learned that the administration had temporarily moved the café to the basement in order to make some repairs to the bar. Reasonable enough, if annoying, I thought. At least I could still get coffee. I bounded down to the bottom floor, two steps at a time, quickened by my anticipation of caffeine. Down in this nether region, a labyrinth of long and narrow storage rooms with dingy lighting and dirty floors stretched out from the main hallway. Peeking into the open, seemingly unattended, yet forbidden rooms, one glimpsed the unending chaos that was Egypt's sacred national heritage: teetering stacks of registers and boxes, mounds of files and paper.

A move from the salubrious second-floor atrium to the muggy basement signified a demotion in the architectural hierarchy of the archive. The siblings rightly took this relocation personally, as a diminution of their status. A week after the move, with no visible beginning on repairs to the bar, the stated reason for their relegation to the basement seemed a pretense. What was happening? The siblings were not sure, but from their perspective, it seemed to be nothing good. Worry and fear settled into their faces. Previously, I had gone to the café to get reenergized by caffeine and the usual cheeriness of the café siblings. Now, our roles reversed: I needed to uplift them. To their credit, Hoda, Maha, Emad, and Samah did their best to recreate as much of the jovial second-floor atmosphere as possible in the dungeon of the basement. They arranged some torn, timeworn chairs from upstairs in a U shape around an old rickety table and fashioned a makeshift bar and kitchen from another table. Citing "safety considerations," the archive's director had forbidden them to take their gas stove to the basement, so Turkish coffee was impossible. With only tea and uncertainty in the basement, my friends were humiliated and anxious.

After their kick downstairs, I found myself spending more time with them, engaging in longer conversations, trying to brighten their spirits. Nothing I or anyone else did seemed to lift their somber mood. On one of my breaks, Maha told me of her engagement to an Egyptian who was living in California and working as a trucker. He had been there for more than a year, trying to save enough money for their wedding and an apartment. They seldom spoke, but she showed me her ring as evidence of their relationship. I wondered what she knew of California and asked if she would ever want to move there, adding that I was from California. She hesitated, clearly not wanting to say anything that might offend. "I'm sure it's great," she offered, but it was too far away from her family and it would be too difficult to start over there.

Two and a half weeks later, the director descended to the basement early one morning to tell the siblings to leave immediately and not come back. Security would see them out. He thanked them for their eight years of service, and, in a final punch to the gut, told them that the archive would be keeping the water boiler and gas stove the family had bought with their own money. As they were not government employees and had no contract, or any social capital or connections, the siblings had no recourse and seemingly no path forward except to acquiesce. And so, at around 10 that morning, they left the archive for the last time.

Egypt's social order, which rewarded thuggery, bribery, and bullying while robbing its most precarious citizens of any possible social, legal, or moral remedy, now counted Hoda, Samah, Maha, Emad, and their family on its list of casualties. I was upset when I heard the news that our friends had been so unceremoniously kicked out. I did my best to piece together what I could, but information proved difficult to acquire, as it so often was in Egypt. Some said the siblings had quit. Others told me they had been shown the door because the archive had hired a professional catering company to operate the café.

In addition to the loss of the siblings' cheerful presence, I felt the absence of the family's caffeine supply immediately and acutely. Sitting in the reading room slogging through documents without the aid of a quick pick-me-up or a little break in the café proved daunting. I knew that a good liberal American should care more about his friends who had just lost their jobs than about his need—okay, desire—for coffee, and I did, and yet . . . For the first few days after the family was ejected, I could not last long after lunch and left early. I then tried leaving the building to get my caffeine fix. What had been a half hour of coffee and pleasant conversation with friends just outside the reading room transformed into an ordeal of at least an hour: a ten-minute walk in the heat to and from a crowded café, the security rigmarole of leaving and reentering the building, all to sit alone with a cup of barely passable coffee.

After about three weeks, a researcher colleague and I arranged to pay the family a visit, to express our gratitude for all they had done for us and our outrage at their unfair treatment. We had collected some cash among the researchers and wanted to deliver that, too. My friend knew roughly how to get to the neighborhood of their apartment, so one day after work we went together in my car to Bulaq al-Dakrur, an area that until recently had been part of Cairo's vast rural hinterland. The expanding city had swallowed up this historic farmland, so that, driving along, we passed large concrete apartment blocks interspersed with fields, small irrigation ditches, and animals. Most of the roads were unpaved, with other infrastructure and social services basic at best. It took about forty-five minutes to reach Bulaq al-Dakrur from the archive. My friend navigated, calling Samah every so often to make sure we were headed in the right direction. We arranged to rendezvous with the eldest brother—the one who had not worked in the café—at a large intersection so that he could lead us the rest of the way to their flat through the dense unmarked streets. Samah had given us his phone number, and we told him what kind of car we were driving—my aunt's white Corolla, which I was borrowing while she was working in Saudi Arabia. We found him, and he got in the back seat to direct us the rest of the way. We parked and bought some candy and snacks from a street kiosk for the young children of the married sister, who was visiting from the south.

When we reached the threshold of their apartment on the third floor, our friends greeted us warmly. Clearly still smarting, they seemed genuinely happy to see us. They insisted on making us our favorite coffees and generously prepared them for us, as difficult as that must have been for them. We asked how they were doing and relayed regards from others in the archive. They presented a brave face, recounting how they had first come to work in the archive, their devotion over the years, and how unfairly they had been treated at the end: told to leave immediately and without question, threatened with security, their water boiler and gas stove stolen from them. Samah told us about the rumors that the director had kicked them out so he could offer the café to a friend of his in the hospitality industry who had wanted to take it over for more than a year. Booting out Samah and her siblings thus benefited the director, as it allowed him to strengthen his social ties with one of his businessman friends—a favor he could call in later. Of course, as Samah said, he did not care about her or her family. Without work, Emad had grown deeply depressed, could not sleep, and refused to eat. Their mother told us about the high cost of her diabetes medication. The sister from the south was pregnant, an occasion of real joy but also a source of added financial stress. Securing a job in Cairo is a difficult endeavor for anyone. For individuals of the family's class and educational background, without many connections, it proved especially challenging. Sadly, but alas not surprisingly, none of the siblings had found a new job in the weeks since they had left the archive. After a few hours, we said goodbye to our despondent and indignant friends. The eldest brother walked us back to the car. We gave him the envelope of cash we had collected. He protested; we insisted.

I dropped off my friend at a bus stop and tried to navigate back to my apartment. My thought was to retrace the route we had taken, but I soon found myself on streets I did not recognize and then cemented in traffic. This standstill surpassed even Cairo's high standards. Cars inched to squeeze into every scrap of space until there was no more inching to be done. Obviously going nowhere, I copied my beleaguered fellow motorists and turned off my car's engine to sit motionless for twenty minutes. Exhausted, sweaty in the Cairo summer, frustrated with the traffic and a social system that hurt people so callously, getting more and more agitated by this seemingly never-ending traffic jam, I took the rash move, inspired by others, of making a U-turn. Mind you, there was no lane in which to make a U-turn, so I drove onto and over the long unbroken median, scratching the car's chassis on the concrete as I turned into still heavy but at least flowing traffic to head in the opposite direction, not sure where exactly it would take me.

Thoroughly lost by this point, I assumed that I was likely heading farther from my apartment. I stopped numerous times to ask for help, receiving wildly contradictory directions. Soon I was cursing the world—Egypt, class, my liberal sensibilities, other drivers, everything that had gotten me here. To my left burned a pile of garbage. To my right, three large Nile water buffaloes stared at me, their eyes asking me, as I was asking myself, "What are you doing here?" A reasonable question, given the circumstances. Such moments of distress, at least for me, easily lead to an interrogation of all of one's life decisions, indeed, one's entire existence. What *am* I doing here? Why was I in Egypt in the first place? How was it that my life to this point had resulted in me being surrounded by burning garbage and water buffaloes? What poor life choices had I made? Something had clearly gone askew. What did any of this have to do with becoming a historian?

A sudden lurch of traffic juddered me out of my head, existential crisis temporarily abated. I limped along, I hoped, toward my apartment. Before this hope could fully take hold, the streets coagulated once more. Back in my head, I thought seriously about abandoning the car for the quicker pace of walking. Was I foolish for going to see my friends who had been kicked out of the archive? What had motivated me? Was it a self-righteous attempt to prove something to myself about how human I am, how caring? Who was I kidding? Did I imagine that I could somehow change Egypt or rescue people from the inequities of their circumstances? The kind of injustice visited upon Samah, Hoda, Maha, and Emad occurred a thousand times a day in Egypt, in a thousand places, in a thousand different ways. Was the same social order that structurally oppressed my friends now colluding with Egyptian traffic to teach me a lesson by trapping me on a dirt road of noxious fumes and beasts of burden? Should historians know their privilege and check their conscience at the archive door? Could studying the past produce social justice? Had my doubts about this led me to seek out means of overcoming hardship that were beyond those of the historian, hence my concern about my friends from the café? Why was a decaffeinated, occasionally self-righteous, normally selfish historian, implicated by his class status in the economic struggles of not just one family but many, writing the history of Egypt? Should he be?

After a few hours lost in my thoughts and in the city, I finally found my way back to my apartment. Exhausted and demoralized, I decided to stay home the next day. In fact, it took me a couple of days to return to the archive.

About a month after the siblings were sent packing, a catering company took over the archive's café. Its employees wore black pants, white dress shirts, black vests, and black bow ties. They were professionals. Like their outfits, their cups were uniform, not the hodgepodge we used to enjoy. The company offered chic new drinks like Nescafé cappuccinos made with a frother, a variety of "freesh" juices, and an expanded assortment of snacks. They covered the four broken glass tables with blue polyester tablecloths. Most researchers and staff considered the new café an improvement, cleaner and more professional than the old one, more "brestigious" (prestigious), as Egyptians like to say. Did it make them feel important to be served by someone in a bow tie and uniform rather than by a teenage boy in jeans, a T-shirt, and plastic sandals? If the topic ever came up—which it rarely did—no one seemed very interested in what had happened to that boy, his siblings, or their poor family. Caring was, after all, a luxury.

11

Royalty

Suzanne Mubarak, Egypt's first lady for thirty years, stood as the second highest authority in the country after her husband and unquestionably its most powerful woman. She could replace government ministers with a single gesture, change laws with a phone call, and completely revamp state policy on a whim. She often represented Egypt at international conferences and meetings on subjects ranging from human rights, children, and women's rights to the press, health, and reading. As they did with her husband, Egyptians sometimes admired and always feared her.

In the early spring of 2006, rumors began circulating in the archive that Mrs. Mubarak herself—often affectionately known, like Diana or Oprah, just as Suzy—planned a visit to inaugurate an initiative to create a digital catalog of the entire collection that could be searched by multiple fields. No comprehensive catalog, print or electronic, had ever existed in the archive. In addition to compiling a catalog, the project aimed to make scans of original documents, both to preserve them from damage by human hands and to allow for more open and expedient research. A friend and I agreed to translate some copy for the archive's website from Arabic to English to explain the new electronic system and procedures for accessing the collection. If all the plans we translated materialized, parts of the archive would be available online and researchers could potentially access them without even setting foot in Egypt, without the experience of the reading room, without ever meeting Madam Amal.

Such a fundamental change in the logic and operation of the archive served as the immediate and important reason for Suzy's visit, proving the twinned meaning of *arche:* an origin for knowing and an arena of brute power. The archive's massive undertaking possessed many names, each more ominous than the next: the numerical transition (*al-tahawwul al-raqami*), the mechanization (*al-maykena*), and—the most general and baleful—the system (*al-sistem*). Madam Amal proclaimed proudly, but also forebodingly, that soon everything would "enter the system."

When the rumors started, no one knew when Suzy would arrive. Imminently, we were promised. I asked a few times and was told "next week" and "in a little bit." One of the security guards told me that the movements and public appearances of Suzy and her husband always remained secret until the last possible moment for reasons of national security. This was, after all, the first lady of the largest country in the Middle East. So that Suzy's security detail could inspect and ensure the safety of the building and the area around it, researchers were instructed that there would be no work for two days before her visit and, naturally, on the day itself. By the logic of Egyptian security, historians in the primary repository of Egypt's history represented a risk. What is an archive without historians? More storage container than active, germinating home of historical research. Did Egypt need historians? Not more than it needed Suzy. Security always trumped history, and in the age of the Mubaraks, Egypt's present would always be prioritized over its past. A history of the past few decades—of the dubious means surrounding the Mubaraks' rise to power, their record of corruption and repression, the state's reliance on violence and imprisonment—was indeed threatening. Forget what was or what could be (a future without the Mubaraks). Only now existed. Like the itinerary of Suzy's visit, Egypt did not need to know anything about the before or after. The immediacy of the present extinguished anything else.

The pollution of Africa's largest city had long ago besmirched the archive's cream-colored façade and interior white walls and marble floors, making the building look and feel exactly as an archive should: old and dingy, shabby and dirty. The reading room needed some general cleaning and refurbishment. Many of its lights flickered or had burned out, stains discolored the walls, the greenish-gray carpet was frayed and badly torn, the old wooden desks creaked and cracked, and many of the chairs had splintered. None of this presented much of a problem for us researchers and most government employees, the reading room's primary denizens. We found it all more than adequate. From the perspective of the archive's administration and the few others who cared to consider the issue, researchers and bureaucrats did not need anything too nice anyway.

For Suzy, however, this was entirely unacceptable. A complete—even if temporary—makeover was required to render the reading room suitable as a stage for the drama of the Suzy visit. The time she would spend in the very front of the room—likely less than five minutes—would prove the most consequential hundreds of seconds in the reading room's entire history. If she found anything unpleasing, she could fire the director of the archive, the Minister of Culture, or anyone else she liked (save her husband); she could order the entire edifice demolished and a new one built in its stead; or she could decree that Egypt had no use for an archive at all. Like Madam Amal under normal circumstances in the reading room, Suzy exercised limitless and limitlessly indiscriminate power—hers across the whole of Egypt.

The refurbishment of the reading room started simply enough. Its muted peach walls, bland yet oddly cheery, needed repainting. One morning, I entered as I always did and headed first to place my research permit in the box in front of Madam Amal. Many of the long desks that had lined the walls near the door now stood clustered together in the middle of the entryway, obstructing the path to Madam Amal's desk. My fellow researchers and I were told that this had been done to allow painters access to the entire length of the wall. More than a week passed before they appeared. To flex his authority, the government employee overseeing the contracted painters had ordered the desks to be bunched together long before the painters, who were working in other parts of the building, would arrive.

Painters, plumbers, electricians, and the like never work alone in Egypt. At least two repairmen undertake any job: the person using the tools and his assistant, who carries equipment and hands him things when prompted. Depending on the task, the group can be quite large. Five painters worked in the reading room. Two held brushes, applying paint to the walls. A third mixed the paint, and the other two divided their time between sitting on the neatly folded drop cloths and going in and out of the room. All of them spoke loudly and constantly about matters related and unrelated to the painting. At times, they shouted back and forth between inside and outside the room. Their cell phones rang with Quranic verses and pop songs. Neither Madam Amal nor anyone else asked them to lower their voices or to silence their phones. They were here for Suzy; did we forget? We all, it seemed, were here for Suzy. Sacrifice was required. Over the course of a week of potent smells and constant noise, most of us researchers—a few could not stand it—continued coming in every day to do what history we could. Something, after all, seemed better than nothing.

When the painting finished, all was quiet for a few days. The smell dissipated, the walls shimmered their new peachy color, and we returned to our normal cadence of reading and transcribing. The room indeed felt refreshed, but surely painting could not be the end of things. Suzy demanded more than just a fresh coat of paint. Although we expected more, no one knew what would come or when. What was the plan? Was there a plan? As with the date of Suzy's visit and in so many other realms of Egyptian society, the control of time and the strategic withholding of knowledge structured the power dynamics of the archive. A research permit could come in six weeks or seven months. The archive might close four hours early today, without warning and with no reason given. To further their power in a world of opaque information, those who knew why and when certain things would happen kept this knowledge to themselves, only choosing to disclose it at strategic moments and for self-interested purposes.

In both the Egyptian present and the Egyptian past, therefore, historians operate with only fragmentary information. In the archival sea, historians search for scraps of paper that give up clues only now and then, and perhaps not any material one needs or wants. With incomplete evidence, the historian pieces these fragments together to offer a picture of how the world worked. The subjective narrativization of these common materials by historians of different interests, abilities, biases, and training is what produces a diverse set of sometimes conflicting conclusions about the past. In much the same way, as the preparations for Suzy's visit progressed, my fellow researchers and I, as the least important, most expendable class in the archive, received only piecemeal, stray, and contradictory information, each of us interpreting it in our own way as we threaded together a story about our collective present that made sense to us as individuals based on our experience, credulity, and imagination. We never knew if the next day would be a day of refurbishments, workers, and yelling, or one of calm study. We had to decide for ourselves what to believe. Yesterday and today projected nothing about tomorrow. Would the archive even open? Asking Madam Amal, who might know, would seldom yield an answer and would only serve to solidify and bolster her power over us. "Come tomorrow and check," she would obfuscate, or, even more unpromisingly, "Don't worry—everything will hopefully be fine."

One morning at 11 a.m., the reading room suddenly went dark. Startled for a moment, I realized that it was just a power cut, a common enough occurrence in Cairo. The keeper of knowledge, possessor of might, Madam Amal, it quickly became apparent, had known exactly when the electricity would go out that day. She had collected her personal belongings on the desk in front of her, ready to depart in an instant. The moment the lights went out, she stood up, grabbed her purse, and told us all to get up; the day was over. Time to go, no more registers or documents, hurry up. Electricians were doing some work in preparation for Suzy's visit, and the electricity would be off for the rest of the day—a situation that clearly thrilled Madam Amal as it meant an abbreviated workday. As we left the room, we stumbled in the dark, some complaining, others excited to have a legitimate excuse to cut their work short. We were instructed to return the next day, when the electricity would be back on, when everything would hopefully be fine. Don't worry.

The next day, we found that the electricity had indeed been restored. As we settled down to work, further plans took shape in front of us. Late that morning, the director of the archive appeared in the reading room with two men in suits. Important markers of class and social status, reserved for businessmen, government officials, and professionals—or those *pretending* to be businessmen, government officials, and professionals—suits presaged major developments. The director said something to Madam Amal when he entered the room, and then the three men walked around examining the walls and ceiling, weighing the relative advantages and disadvantages of each location. It was not clear to me what they were discussing. Something to do with the electricity again? New light fixtures? The three men left, and about an hour later the two men in suits returned with a group of seven or eight men in work coveralls carrying large spools of cable, white plastic, and some electrical equipment. After about an hour of these men laying out cable on the floor and shouting to one another across the room, it became clear what they had come to do: they were implementing "the mechanization" (al-maykena), wiring the reading room for the incipient computer network. Ports for network connections would allow researchers to access the online catalog and collections from every one of the room's twenty-four desks.

Wiring the room proved a massive undertaking. For the next eight days, I learned much more about installing a computer network than I did about Egyptian social relations in the eighteenth century. One first needed to determine where to mount the main controls of the network, a panel of switches and servers. This brain of the operation had to be easily accessible and yet protected from any possibility of tampering. I now understood that this was what the director and the two men in suits had been discussing. They decided on a place across from Madam Amal's desk, near some shelves. From this hub, hundreds of feet of cable would fan out to multiple network connections, a series of white plastic housings drilled into the base of the room's walls and many columns. Eight days of teeth-shattering drilling through plastic into drywall, with bonus shouting, resulted in lines and clumps of white plastic pocking the base of nearly every vertical surface, like a pasty mold creeping up from the floor. Not all the cable ran along the floor. Workers threaded some from the central hub above the ceiling tiles and then down the columns, using ladders and even standing on our desks, stepping on our notebooks and a few times even on centuries-old archival material. In one instance, a court register from the seventeenth century was trampled and torn by a muddy work boot. No electronic catalog of the archive's collection yet existed. Would a catalog and computers ever truly materialize?

Answers soon arrived. About three weeks after the reading room was wired, a huge commotion burst through the doors. As if Caesar were processing through Rome, a phalanx of workers I had never seen before trundled in a line of creaky carts carrying large boxes of electronics. A group of five or six higher-up bureaucrats shadowed them, barking instructions. Once inside the reading room, the higher-ups ordered the cargo to be lifted off the contraptions and placed on the floor. The workers dropped the containers with a thud and little regard for their precious contents. The senior bureaucrats then tore into the boxes, informing the workers that they were forbidden to open them since they could not possibly fathom the weighty responsibility of what was inside nor did they possess the requisite technical expertise.

After slashing through cardboard and an impressive amount of plastic packaging and then wading through a flood of Styrofoam and bubble wrap, the bureaucrats surfaced, beaming with pride as they held a computer high for all to behold before bestowing it on a desk. This process was repeated twenty-five times, as every researcher's desk, in addition to Madam Amal's, received a computer. The romantic vision of the patient, meticulous professional historian working quietly in the archive stood in stark contrast to the scene playing out in the reading room that day. Each desk rose as an island of fixity from a raging sea of bubble wrap and flying cardboard. The words of archival texts competed with the voices of archival bureaucrats yelling at one another to lift, be careful, and hurry up. As researchers read, bureaucrats positioned computers on their desks as if they were not there. The functionaries pondered the relative merits of different layouts for each computer setup, sometimes screeching a machine from one side of a desk to another. Should the processor go on the floor or sit on the desk? Was it too far away from the cable connection? Would it be better for the monitor to be in the center of the desk or to one side? Where to position the mouse? Of course, no one consulted the researchers, who would be the ones using the computers, about the most optimal arrangement. The computers remained unplugged while those who had pushed the carts into the room followed orders to clean up the mess their superiors had created.

The director returned to inspect the reading room, which now boasted a computer on every desk. Eager to please their boss, the higher-up bureaucrats reported their achievement, relaying how they had transported the computers and explaining the thinking behind the position of the computer on each desk. The director listened. What he cared most about was how best to display the newly computerized reading room to Suzy (always "First Lady Suzanne Mubarak" to him) during her visit. Props in position, how to stage the play? Would it be desirable to have a researcher working at each computer when Suzy came into the room? Should there be a select group of "real" researchers or, since historians were inherently untrustworthy, members of the archive's staff posing as researchers? Should all the computers be turned on or just some? Should they invite the first lady to use one of the computers? Or was this too risky, since a computer could be slow or not work properly? In the mid-2000s, computers remained new enough in Egypt to promise exciting possibilities even as they provoked nervousness and fear.

The network panel installed on the wall across from Madam Amal's desk proved a source of much discussion. It flashed in all sorts of colors and looked impressively technical; it flickered as the blinking jewel in the newly wired reading room's crown. The director devoted laser focus to ensuring that Suzy would see it, to demonstrate to her that the archive—*his* archive (really hers)—pushed at the forefront of the archival sciences with the latest technology. Given the panel's position away from the door and around a corner, however, someone only glancing quickly into the reading room, as all assumed Suzy would, might easily miss it. One needed to walk a significant distance into the room to see the panel. Suzy would ultimately do what Suzy wanted to do, but, hoping to predict her moves, the director and some of the higher-up bureaucrats enacted the moment she would enter the room, tracing out the possible routes she might take from the door, debating the relative merits of each, choreographing each step with a precision and care rarely witnessed in the archive.

Over the next few days, the archive's maintenance staff removed the reading room's windows and took them to be hosed off, scoured, and dried before returning them to their casings. New blinds appeared over the freshly washed windows. The carpet received a thorough cleaning, the air conditioning units worked more efficiently after a long-overdue dusting, and the desks were rearranged in a fetching new shamrock pattern. It had been nearly two months since the first rumors of Suzy's visit prompted the exuberant refurbishments, but still there was no word of when exactly she would come. The director had done all he could to improve the reading room. Painted, wired, networked, and cleaned, the room now gleamed for its presentation to Suzy. But this state of readiness cast against the uncertainty of her arrival stirred feelings of anxious urgency. The luxurious condition of the reading room would surely not last long. From this immaculate pinnacle, the only possibility was deterioration.

Without knowing when (if?) Suzy would arrive, we were told that the Minister of Culture would soon visit to inspect the archive's preparations personally. Obviously nowhere near the stature of Suzy, the Minister of Culture still towered as an enormous figure; he held the highest direct authority over the archive, just a notch or two under Suzy and her husband. On a Sunday, word arrived that he would come that Wednesday and that it would be a normal workday.

Apart from a clamoring buzz and dressed-up bureaucrats sprinting to attend to last-minute details, Wednesday did indeed operate as a regular day in the archive. I arrived, checked myself and my things in, and sat down to work. At about 11:30, Madam Amal received the call that the minister had arrived. She announced the news to all of us, instructing us to get ready. It was not clear what that meant. Ready for what? Excitement grew in the reading room. I felt it, too; it was hard not to. After waiting all morning, really for months since word of Suzy's visit had first circulated, we were finally hosting a guest of honor—not the one we were expecting, but still a minister,

important in his own right and also because his appearance
boded well for Suzy's eventual arrival. Some researchers continued to work, while others stood waiting anxiously for the
minister. Although he was now in the building, no one knew
the agenda for his visit because of the politics of security and
information, and therefore no one knew if he would even come
to the reading room. In the end, no matter his slated itinerary,
he could choose to see and ignore whatever he liked.

About an hour after the announcement of his arrival, the
minister did indeed enter the reading room, surrounded by
a huge entourage of people in suits, including the director of
the archive and two photographers. The director introduced
the minister to Madam Amal and her staff behind the front
desk. Madam Amal smiled and greeted the minister with the
complete deference she knew to show him. The minister then
glanced around the shining clean room. The director told him
about the computers and the new network. He saw the backs
of the turned-off computers. Did he notice the researchers sitting behind the computers? Camera bulbs flashed. The director then led the minister in the ballet he had plotted from the
door to the glittering panel on the wall that had been the subject of so much discussion. The pas de deux succeeded flaw-
lessly on this day, auguring well for Suzy's visit. After less than
three minutes in the reading room, the whole group turned
and left.

An archive employee, a friend of mine, told me the next
day that the minister had generally been pleased with the archive's state of preparedness. Because nothing could be completely acceptable, however, he issued one important directive.
He found the white and black marble floors throughout the
building embarrassingly feculent and démodé, and he ordered
that they be replaced before Suzy arrived. When I asked my
friend how a project as enormous as destroying and then re-

tiling the four floors of an expansive building could be completed so quickly (after all, Suzy's visit was *clearly* imminent), he assured me that it would be since the minister had ordered it. What a minister decrees happens. There is no discussion. My friend told me that workers would devote twenty-four hours a day to the job and that it would probably be done in a week or so.

After days of jackhammering, banging, and dust (a bit longer than a week in the end), the floors—the final piece of the preparations for Suzy's arrival—stood almost magically remade. But by the summer of 2007—more than a year after rumors of her visit first began and after months of renovations and stress—Suzy still had not come. Some explained that she had been engrossed in a constitutional referendum that spring. Others speculated that the delay in the electronic catalog was keeping her away. Whatever the reason for her nonappearance, we all knew—*knew*—that she would appear any day now. Suzy would come. We had to be alert in our waiting, always ready.

But Suzy did not come. The promised visit of Suzanne Mubarak ultimately went unfulfilled. Despite consuming everyone and everything for over a year, the envisioned event was never recorded; no reference or text about the first lady's visit to the archive exists anywhere in its collection. This episode that forever changed the function of a crucial government institution remains "hidden in the archives," in ways quite different from what we usually mean by this phrase. This chapter of the archive's story illuminates much of the politics of Egypt in the early 2000s that would lead to the revolt of 2011. In this way, despite the archive's lack of any written sources about the political rebellion of 2011, the institution does house its history.

Government officials like Suzy or the Minister of Culture

possessed near absolute power over those beneath them, in the government hierarchy and in society at large, and therefore expected and usually enjoyed near infinite respect and deference. The Mubaraks ruled Egypt like a royal family, and it is no surprise that they became the targets of the 2011 protests that ultimately succeeded in removing them from power. Nevertheless, the exercise of absolute and arbitrary hierarchical power, before and after the Mubaraks, has been so deeply entrenched across Egyptian government bureaucracies—and also across Egyptian companies, families, schools, and most social groups—that cutting off the head does not kill the snake. Egyptians have been acculturated to hierarchical bureaucratic power and its unjust consequences for centuries, some might say millennia. Indubitably, there is nothing inherent in Egypt or Egyptians about this politics; indeed, it breeds widespread animosities and resentments, as 2011 made clear. Still, these ingredients have long been baked into Egypt's social structures, economy, bureaucracy, schools, and families. Overcoming this would therefore require a wholesale remaking of the country, as indeed many in January 2011 aspired to do.

Suzy's announced visit in 2006 enacted the ensconced politics of autocracy so regularized in Egypt. Everything shifted to preparing for her, all other work deemed irrelevant. Who cared about research in an archive? A singular devotion to pleasing the individual ruler monopolized everyone's attention, despite the fact that Suzy might simply poke her head into the reading room or might forgo it altogether: a year of labor, twenty-five new computers, fresh marble, and endless anxiety for minutes, seconds, or none of Suzy's time. But no one questions the orders or wishes of those in positions of power. The head of the archive directed that the reading room be completely remodeled and wired, and so it happened. The minister decreed the floors be resurfaced, and heaven and earth shifted to make it so. If the minister wanted everyone to wear only green every day, everyone would unquestioningly wear only green every day. Arbitrariness serves as a measure of the absoluteness of one's authority. The more illogical, unnecessary, or even detrimental a directive, the more powerful the testament to one's dominance when it is followed.

At the same time, an extraordinary moment such as Suzy's visit presented rare opportunities to impress one's superiors and therefore potentially to disrupt and even rearrange the established hierarchy to one's advantage. At every point in Egypt's seemingly solidified social structure, the person of rank possesses essentially infinite power over the person below and no power in comparison to the person above. One must therefore always dominate down. However, in a high-stakes context such as that surrounding Suzy's visit, if someone of an elevated status fails in his or her charge, someone below can maneuver by proving that his or her abilities better meet the exigent demands of the moment. Doing a job well never produces a reward, but mistakes always give rise to lasting consequences. Madam Amal expects the bureaucrats underneath her to do an effective job of managing the cleaning of the windows. Madam Amal's ability to produce clean windows by controlling her inferiors allows her to maintain her favor with the director of the archive. This in turn will impress the Minister of Culture when he visits the archive, prompting him to commend the director for doing a capable job. And, ultimately, Suzy will be pleased with the work of the minister. In these ways, all preserve the authority of their position within the system. Any leapfrogging that takes advantage of a misstep proves easiest at the lower rungs of the hierarchy; the higher one is, the more mechanisms and structures exist to preserve one's power. At the top, no one could ever outwit Suzy, of course; the entire system buttressed her position. No matter the level in this high-stakes game, if an attempt to best and bypass a superior fails, the consequences may be grave, in fact terminal. This rarely played move rarely succeeds.

Suzy's visit also elucidates how the cadence of time worked as a mode of power in Egypt. All waited for Suzy; indeed, we *rushed* to wait for Suzy. The archive's administration dashed and scrambled to clean and refurbish the building as quickly as possible, ignoring everything else and tolerating whatever noise, smell, and disruption was required. The impressive speed and resolute focus shown throughout the repairs were quickly overtaken by an unspecified wait for a visit that might or might not occur, but one that was most certainly promised. It is this *promise* that in the end matters most. It is power's tool. It elicits the anxiety, fear, and, finally, frustration that Suzy seeks in those she rules. When will she come? Will today be the day? If not today, then surely tomorrow. Like the coming of the Messiah or Hidden Imam: all anticipate, all wait, always ready. Such a politics of delay operates across Egypt. Egyptians are constantly instructed to be patient, to wait only a little bit longer. This happens everywhere: in government offices, in restaurants, at bus stops, in businesses, in traffic, at the hospital, and so on. One waits for pension money, a job, food, democracy, someone to arrive, a kidney. In 2011, Egyptians were done waiting. This was part of the catharsis of the revolt—throwing off the temporal politics of stasis. Suzy wanted us to wait in the archive: wanted to create a degree of expectation, uncertainty, and mystery around her visit; wanted to kindle discussion and suspense; wanted to keep us on edge, in a state of perpetual readiness and hypervigilance. The longer the wait, the stronger her authority, the more impactful her final arrival. For us researchers and bureaucrats, the only possible validation of our waiting, stress, and sacrifice was Suzy's fulfillment of her promise to visit the archive. She forced us to want her to come. Without her arrival, what would it all have been for? And so, in the ultimate show of her power, she never came.

The mere expectation of Suzy's arrival proved metamorphic. The reading room became a much more comfortable place to work. A degree of vigilance and care now held, as we all endeavored to preserve its cleaned and refurbished state. Although the computers sat unused for several more years, boulderlike, eating up space on the desks, and the electronic catalog, when it finally emerged, was incomplete and full of errors—introducing yet one more numbering system and creating more confusion than order—those rickety carts had ushered in a new epoch: the machine age. Researchers no longer relied on conversations with other historians, published citations, or trial and error. The computers changed not only how information made its way through the archive and how researchers related but also the physical layout of the reading room. Instead of our large open desks that allowed for freely flowing greetings, conversations, and visual cues, we now sat at separate cavernous carrels, walled off from one another, staring at screens. The archive had become a far more solitary place.

One aspect of life that stayed the same—even hardened— after the computers arrived was the security regime of surveillance that seeped into everything in the archive. With researchers now logging into computers with usernames and passwords, the archive could much more easily censor and prevent access to materials and collect and store a record of each individual's research activities. The computers automated the archive's hierarchy, its politics of information withholding and distribution, and its policing capabilities. Egypt's fractal power politics that diffused from the Mubaraks down through

government agencies and bureaucrats like Madam Amal operated much more efficiently by machine. We had entered a new
era. Without ever setting foot in the archive, Suzy had transformed it. The reading room's makeover remade the making
of Egyptian history.

12

Credits

This is the first book I ever started writing. The shortest, the most personal, it took me the longest to complete. I began it while in graduate school in the early 2000s and then worked on it in fits and starts, with bursts of energy at different times and in different places: in Berkeley and Cairo, New Haven and Istanbul; as a graduate student and department chair; for a conference at University College London and meetings of the Middle East Studies Association; during a weekend in Ann Arbor; in New York. It carries the marks of twenty years of professional and personal life—temporary moments and lasting relationships with people, texts, institutions, cities, and ideas.

I offer a sense of those intellectual and personal debts here. This is inevitably and intentionally an incomplete autobiobibliography. I will fail to mention people and books, and I am protecting the names of some in Egypt (I have used pseudonyms throughout the preceding text). Evocation of inspiration, not exhaustive acknowledgment, is my goal.

First and forever, thanks to the entire staff of the Egyptian National Archives. Without them, needless to say, this book—and many others—would not exist. I will always be grateful for their patient work and steadfastness, their good humor and resourcefulness. I was endlessly fortunate to share the reading room with a group of enormously talented historians, who have published multiple generations of scholarship. Some of their works, which demonstrate the richness of the archive and which continue to teach me, include Raouf Abbas and Assem El-Dessouky, *The Large Landowning Class and the Peasantry in Egypt, 1837–1952*, translated by Amer Mohsen with Mona Zikri, edited by Peter Gran (Syracuse, N.Y.: Syracuse University Press, 2011); Naṣra ʿAbd al-Mutajallī, "al-Muqāwama bil-Tasaḥḥub fī Rīf Miṣr al-ʿUthmāniyya," in *al-Rafḍ wa al-Iḥtijāj fī al-Mujtamaʿ al-Miṣrī fī al-ʿAṣr al-ʿUthmānī*, edited by Nāṣir Ibrāhīm and Raʾūf ʿAbbās (Cairo: Markaz al-Buḥūth wa al-Dirāsāt al-Ijtimāʿiyya, 2004), 127–36; Ḥusām Muḥammad ʿAbd al-Muʿṭī, *al-ʿAlāqāt al-Miṣriyya al-Ḥijāziyya fī al-Qarn al-Thāmin ʿAshar* (Cairo: al-Hayʾa al-Miṣriyya al-ʿĀmma lil-Kitāb, 1999); Zeinab Abul-Magd, *Imagined Empires: A History of Revolt in Egypt* (Berkeley: University of California Press, 2013); Muḥammad ʿAfīfī, *al-Awqāf wa al-Ḥayāh al-Iqtiṣādiyya fī Miṣr fī al-ʿAṣr al-ʿUthmānī* (Cairo: al-Hayʾa al-Miṣriyya al-ʿĀmma lil-Kitāb, 1991); James E. Baldwin, *Islamic Law and Empire in Ottoman Cairo* (Edinburgh: Edinburgh University Press, 2017); Jennifer L. Derr, *The Lived Nile: Environment, Disease, and Material Colonial Economy in Egypt* (Stanford: Stanford University Press, 2019); Khaled Fahmy, *All the Pasha's Men: Mehmed Ali, His Army, and the Making of Modern Egypt* (Cambridge: Cambridge University Press, 1997); Khaled Fahmy, *In Quest of Justice: Islamic Law and Forensic Medicine in Modern Egypt* (Oakland: University of California Press, 2018); Pascale Ghazaleh, *Masters of the Trade: Crafts and Craftspeople in Cairo, 1750–*

1850, Cairo Papers in Social Science, vol. 22, no. 3 (Cairo: American University in Cairo Press, 1999); Ra'ūf 'Abbās Ḥāmid, *al-
Ḥaraka al-'Ummāliyya fī Miṣr, 1899–1952* (Cairo: Dār al-Kātib
al-'Arabī lil-Ṭibā'a wa al-Nashr, 1967); Will Hanley, *Identifying
with Nationality: Europeans, Ottomans, and Egyptians in Alexandria* (New York: Columbia University Press, 2017); Nelly
Hanna, *Making Big Money in 1600: The Life and Times of Is-
ma'il Abu Taqiyya, Egyptian Merchant* (Syracuse, N.Y.: Syracuse University Press, 1998); Nelly Hanna, *In Praise of Books:
A Cultural History of Cairo's Middle Class, Sixteenth to the Eighteenth Century* (Syracuse, N.Y.: Syracuse University Press, 2003);
'Imād Hilāl, *al-Fallāḥ wa al-Sulṭa wa al-Qānūn: Miṣr fī al-Niṣf
al-Thānī min al-Qarn al-Tāsi' 'Ashar* (Cairo: Dār al-Kutub wa
al-Wathā'iq al-Qawmiyya, 2007); Nāṣir Aḥmad Ibrāhīm, *al-
Azamāt al-Ijtimā'iyya fī Miṣr fī al-Qarn al-Sābi' 'Ashar* (Cairo:
Dār al-Āfāq al-'Arabiyya, 1998); Majdī Jirjis, "al-Qubt wa al-
Muqaddasāt al-Islāmiyya," *al-Rūznāma: al-Ḥauliyya al-Miṣriyya
lil-Wathā'iq* 6 (2008): 111–33; Hanan Kholoussy, *For Better, For
Worse: The Marriage Crisis That Made Modern Egypt* (Stanford: Stanford University Press, 2010); Nicolas Michel, "Migra-
tions de paysans dans le Delta du Nil au début de l'époque
ottoman," *Annales Islamologiques* 35 (2001): 241–90; Nicolas
Michel, "Les rizaq iḥbāsiyya, terres agricoles en mainmorte
dans l'Égypte mamelouke et ottoman. Étude sur les Dafātir
al-Aḥbās ottomans," *Annales Islamologiques* 30 (1996): 105–98;
Shana Minkin, *Imperial Bodies: Empire and Death in Alexandria, Egypt* (Stanford: Stanford University Press, 2020); Lisa Pol-
lard, *Nurturing the Nation: The Family Politics of Modernizing,
Colonizing, and Liberating Egypt, 1805–1923* (Berkeley: University of California Press, 2005); Jīhān 'Umrān, "Wathīqat Kashf
'alā al-Sawāqī wa al-Majrā al-Sulṭānī (Dirāsa Wathā'iqiyya),"
Annales Islamologiques 40 (2006): 1–23; Nāṣir 'Uthmān, "Maḥka-
mat Rashīd ka-Maṣdar li-Dirāsat Tijārat al-Nasīj fī Madīnat

al-Iskandariyya fī al-ʿAṣr al-ʿUthmānī," *al-Rūznāma: al-Ḥauli-yya al-Miṣriyya lil-Wathāʾiq* 3 (2005): 355–85. For more work based on research in the Egyptian National Archives, see articles in the journal *al-Rūznāma: al-Ḥauliyya al-Miṣriyya lil-Wathāʾiq*.

On the history of the archive and for incisive studies about the collection and its place in Egypt, see Lucia Carminati, "Dead Ends In and Out of the Archive: An Ethnography of Dār al Wathāʾiq al Qawmiyya, the Egyptian National Archive," *Rethinking History* 23 (2019): 34–51; Daniel Crecelius, "The Organization of *Waqf* Documents in Cairo," *International Journal of Middle East Studies* 2 (1971): 266–77; Yoav Di-Capua, *Gatekeepers of the Arab Past: Historians and History Writing in Twentieth-Century Egypt* (Berkeley: University of California Press, 2009); Omnia El Shakry, "'History Without Documents': The Vexed Archives of Decolonization in the Middle East," *American Historical Review* 120 (2015): 920–34; Khaled Fahmy, "The Crisis of the Humanities in Egypt," *Comparative Studies of South Asia, Africa, and the Middle East* 37 (2017): 142–48; Hanan Hammad, "Daily Encounters That Make History: History from Below and Archival Collaboration," *International Journal of Middle East Studies* 53 (2021): 139–43; Majdī Jirjis, "Manhaj al-Dirāsāt al-Wathāʾiqiyya wa Wāqiʿ al-Baḥth fī Miṣr," *al-Rūznāma: al-Ḥauliyya al-Miṣriyya lil-Wathāʾiq* 2 (2004): 237–87; Dānyāl Krīsaliyūs, editor, *Fihris Waqfiyyāt al-ʿAṣr al-ʿUthmānī al-Maḥfūẓa bi-Wizārat al-Awqāf wa Dār al-Wathāʾiq al-Tārīkhiyya al-Qawmiyya bil-Qāhira* (Cairo: Dār al-Nahḍa al-ʿArabiyya, 1992); Ibrahım el-Mouelhy, *Organisation et fonctionnement des institutions ottomanes en Egypte (1517–1917): etude documentaire, d'après les sources archivistiques égyptiennes* (Ankara [?]: Imprimerie de la Société turque d'histoire, 1989); Hussein Omar, "The State of the Archive: Manipulating Memory in Modern Egypt and the Writing of Egyptological Histories," in *Histories of Egyptology: Interdisciplinary Measures,* edited by William Carruthers (New York: Routledge, 2015), 174–84; Asad J. Rustom, *The Royal Archives of Egypt and the Origins of the Egyptian Expedition to Syria, 1831–1841* (Beirut: American Press, 1936); Stanford J. Shaw, "Cairo's Archives and the History of Ottoman Egypt," *Middle East Institute Report on Current Research* (1956): 59–72; 'Abd al-Wudūd Yūsif, "Sijillāt al-Maḥākim al-Shar'iyya ka-Maṣdar Asāsī li-Tārīkh al-'Arab fī al-'Aṣr al-'Uthmānī," *Egyptian Historical Review* 19 (1972): 325–35.

On the intersections of the 2011 rebellion and archival politics in Egypt, begin with the gargantuan video library of the Mosireen Collective: www.mosireen.com. See also Khaled Fahmy, "Ministry of Culture or Ministry of Intellectuals?," *Ahram Online,* June 8, 2013; Khaled Fahmy, "Mr. Minister, What Are You Talking About?," *Ahram Online,* June 23, 2013; Khaled Fahmy, "Who Is Afraid of the National Archives?," *Ahram Online,* June 16, 2013; Pascale Ghazaleh, "Past Imperfect, Future Tense: Writing People's Histories in the Middle East Today," *Essays of the Forum Transregionale Studien* 5 (Berlin: Forum Transregionale Studien, 2019); Joshua Hersh, "The Battle of the Archives: What Egypt's Intellectuals Lost," *New Yorker,* September 4, 2013; Hussein Omar, "Who Should Save Egypt's Archives?," *Al Jazeera,* January 25, 2012; Amir-Hussein Radjy, "How to Save the Memories of the Egyptian Revolution," *Atlantic,* January 25, 2018; Lucie Ryzova, "New Asymmetries in the New Authoritarianism: Research in Egypt in the Age of Post-Revolution," *International Journal of Middle East Studies* 49 (2017): 511–14.

Over the past twenty years, the following books helped me to understand what this one could and should be: Timothy Garton Ash, *The File: A Personal History* (New York: Random House, 1997); Antoinette Burton, editor, *Archive Stories: Facts,*

Fictions, and the Writing of History (Durham, N.C.: Duke University Press, 2005); Robert A. Caro, *Working: Researching, Interviewing, Writing* (New York: Alfred A. Knopf, 2019); Steven C. Caton, *Yemen Chronicle: An Anthropology of War and Mediation* (New York: Hill and Wang, 2005); Bernard S. Cohn, *An Anthropologist Among the Historians and Other Essays* (Delhi: Oxford University Press, 1987); Natalie Zemon Davis, *Fiction in the Archives: Pardon Tales and Their Tellers in Sixteenth-Century France* (Stanford: Stanford University Press, 1987); Arlette Farge, *The Allure of the Archives,* translated by Thomas Scott-Railton (New Haven: Yale University Press, 2013); Clifford Geertz, *Works and Lives: The Anthropologist as Author* (Stanford: Stanford University Press, 1988); Amitav Ghosh, *In an Antique Land* (New York: Vintage, 1994); Carlo Ginzburg, *Threads and Traces: True, False, Fictive,* translated by Anne C. Tedeschi and John Tedeschi (Berkeley: University of California Press, 2012); Anthony Grafton, *The Footnote: A Curious History* (Cambridge, Mass.: Harvard University Press, 1997); Clara Han, *Seeing Like a Child: Inheriting the Korean War* (New York: Fordham University Press, 2021); Saidiya Hartman, *Wayward Lives, Beautiful Experiments: Intimate Histories of Social Upheaval* (New York: W. W. Norton, 2019); Matthew S. Hull, *Government of Paper: The Materiality of Bureaucracy in Urban Pakistan* (Berkeley: University of California Press, 2012); Timothy Pachirat, *Among Wolves: Ethnography and the Immersive Study of Power* (New York: Routledge, 2018); Anand Pandian and Stuart McLean, editors, *Crumpled Paper Boat: Experiments in Ethnographic Writing* (Durham, N.C.: Duke University Press, 2017); Theodore K. Rabb and Robert I. Rotberg, editors, *The New History: The 1980s and Beyond* (Princeton: Princeton University Press, 1982); Paul Rabinow, *Reflections on Fieldwork in Morocco* (Berkeley: University of California Press, 1977); Samer S. Shehata, *Shop Floor Culture and Politics*

in Egypt (Albany: State University of New York Press, 2009);
Jonathan D. Spence, *The Question of Hu* (New York: Alfred A.
Knopf, 1988); Michael Taussig, *My Cocaine Museum* (Chicago:
University of Chicago Press, 2004).

I learned about the meanings of *arche* and archive from
Angela Garcia, "The Ambivalent Archive," in *Crumpled Paper
Boat*, 29–44, and Angela Garcia, "The Blue Years: An Ethnography of a Prison Archive," *Cultural Anthropology* 31 (2016):
571–94. The quote from Michel de Certeau in the first para-
graph of this book comes from *The Writing of History*, translated by Tom Conley (New York: Columbia University Press,
1988), 77.

I humbly and profusely thank Khaled Fahmy for all he
made possible. He helped me wade into and understand the
archives and taught me more about them and Egyptian history
than anyone else. As the above citations attest, he is a historian's historian, and he has argued passionately for the role of
the archive and for the place of history generally in Egyptian
society. Zeinab Abul-Magd, Jennifer L. Derr, Angie Heo, Al-
legra Huston, and Kathryn Lofton each read a full draft of this
book and offered incisive critiques and productive suggestions.
I thank them and the authors of the two anonymous reviews so-
licited by Yale University Press. Additionally, Omnia El Shakry,
Amira Mittermaier, Mara Naaman, and Paul Rabinow com-
mented on and improved parts of this work at various points
over the years. Elizabeth Casey, Jaya Chatterjee, Phillip King,
Eva Skewes, and Wendy Strothman helped to bring it into the
world. I am grateful to Stephen R. Latham of the Yale University Institutional Review Board for his instruction. Of course,
full responsibility for this text lies only with me.

Mary R. Welch makes the world inside and outside of
books infinitely better. What good fortune is mine to have her
in my life.